peanut butter
planet

peanut butter planet

around the world in 80 recipes, from starters to main dishes to desserts

robin robertson photography by mark ferri

RODALE

Printed in the United States of America
Rodale Inc. makes every effort to use acid-free ∞, recycled paper ♻.

Cover photo: Homemade Peanut Butter, page 8, by Mark Ferri

Photographs by Mark Ferri

Book design by Carol Angstadt

Library of Congress Cataloging-in-Publication Data

Robertson, Robin (Robin G.)
    Peanut butter planet : around the world in 80 recipes, from starters to
main dishes to desserts / Robin Robertson.
        p.   cm.
    Includes index.
    ISBN-13 978-1-57954-963-3 paperback
    ISBN-10 1-57954-963-2 paperback
    1. Cookery (Peanut butter)   2. Cookery, International.   I. Title.
TX814.5.P38R63 2006
641.6'56596—dc22   2005030660

Distributed to the trade by Holtzbrinck Publishers

2 4 6 8 10 9 7 5 3 1 paperback

RODALE
LIVE YOUR WHOLE LIFE™

We inspire and enable people to improve their lives and the world around them
For more of our products visit **rodalestore.com** or call 800-848-4735

for stacey

contents

acknowledgments

My heartfelt gratitude goes to my recipe testers and fellow peanut butter lovers: Gloria Siegel, Laura Frisk, Christina O'Brien, Linda Elsenbaumer, Troy Seidle, Lori Kettler, Robyn Wesley, Hannah and Philip Schein, and Janet Aaronson. Much appreciation goes to my husband, Jon Robertson, for his help as an enthusiastic taster of all things peanut butter and for helping me keep my computer files organized. Thanks also to Simone Gabbay, Jannette Patterson, and Kelli Polsinelli, as well as the National Peanut Board. A very special thank-you goes to my agent, Stacey Glick of Dystel and Goderich Literary Management, for suggesting that I write this book. I also want to thank everyone at Rodale who made this book a reality, especially Pamela Adler, Miriam Backes, and Margot Schupf.

introduction

Like most people, my personal odyssey with peanut butter began in childhood with the frequent appearance of those sturdy sandwiches in my lunch box. I never grew tired of them and sometimes requested one when my mother prepared something I didn't like for dinner. My love of peanut butter soon extended to sweets, with peanut butter cookies and those decadent chocolate–peanut butter cups topping my list of favorite confections.

Unfortunately, the calorie counting and fat-gram monitoring of adulthood condemned my beloved spread to the shelf for a time. As I learned more about international cuisines, however, I discovered that peanut butter is used as a cooking ingredient throughout the world. I soon began looking at my old friend in a new light and realized that since the flavor of peanut butter is so intense, a little goes a long way. Just a small amount is needed to enliven sauces, soups, and other savory dishes. Soon after this discovery, a wonderful thing happened: Medical science revealed that peanut butter, like olive oil, contains monounsaturated fats and is therefore good for you. Monounsaturated fats have been found to actually help lower cholesterol and improve heart function.

Inspired by those discoveries and fueled by my passion for peanut butter, the idea for this book was born. *Peanut Butter Planet* will help you become reacquainted with your old lunch-box companion too, so you can enjoy a variety of familiar and exotic recipes that range far beyond the beloved American sandwich.

AN AMERICAN TRADITION

Peanut butter has been a favorite kitchen staple in American homes ever since the 1904 St. Louis World's Fair, where it was first introduced (concession stands sold it for one penny per serving). During the 20th century, it was reserved mainly for sandwiches, confections, and the occasional roving finger or spoon. These days, however, health-conscious Americans have rediscovered peanut butter as an easy and delicious way to add protein-rich flavor to their meals and a great way to include more healthy fat in their diets. Not only is it a nutritional powerhouse—with fiber, niacin, magnesium, B-complex vitamins, copper, and folate (in addition to protein)—but it is convenient and inexpensive too. No wonder peanut butter is America's favorite comfort food.

Some people might dismiss peanut butter as "kid's stuff," but virtually everyone has a jar on hand to appease the child within—whether to make the iconic sandwich or perhaps indulge in one of life's guilty pleasures: dipping a spoon (or finger) directly into the jar at midnight.

We all eat peanut butter. Parents turn to it to nourish fussy kids. Young singles and families alike crave it as a delicious and economical protein source, as do the more than 12 million vegetarians in the United States and other health-conscious people. Whether they enjoy it as a snack, as part of a meal, or as dessert, Americans have a love affair with peanut butter.

Centuries before peanut butter made its first public appearance in the United States, it was a staple in Asia, Africa, and South America for soups, stews, sauces, salads, and main dishes. However, it was not referred to as peanut butter in these other countries, but was simply peanuts ground to a paste (much as we would make our own homemade peanut butter). In fact, more than 90 percent of the world's peanuts are grown in Africa and Asia. Peanut butter was first developed in the United States during the 1890s as a high-protein health food. Dr. John Harvey Kellogg (the Kellogg's cereal magnate) initially developed peanut butter as a meat alternative for his patients, and was the first to patent the product.

CHOICES, CHOICES

"Crunchy" and "smooth" aren't the only choices to make among the varieties of peanut butter. We can also choose between "all natural" and "regular." Specialty peanut butters are available as well, including those that have "stripes" of jelly blended right in the jar. By law, commercial peanut butters must contain 90 percent peanuts.

The incredible silky, spreadable consistency of regular peanut butter is due to the hydrogenated vegetable oils that are added after the peanuts are roasted, blanched, and ground. These added oils act as stabilizers and prevent the peanut oil from separating from the spread. In terms of freshness and flavor, however, nothing beats freshly ground peanut butter. Some natural food stores will grind it while you wait. It is also simple to make your own peanut butter at home in a blender or food processor. Recipes for homemade peanut butter are provided on page 8.

NUTRITIONAL VALUE

Like its leguminous relatives (peanuts are not nuts, but legumes), peanut butter is rich in protein, fiber, vitamins, and essential fatty acids. Although peanut butter contains about 50 percent fat, it is mostly unsaturated. At about 26 percent protein, peanut butter is also an excellent source of B-complex vitamins as well as potassium, magnesium, calcium, and iron. Studies have shown that regularly eating foods rich in unsaturated fat can actually help lower blood cholesterol levels. Peanut butter is also naturally cholesterol-free. Its intense flavor means a little can go a long way, and because it is low in cost, it is an economical protein source. One delicious way to reduce saturated fat intake is to use peanut butter as a replacement for the butter or margarine that's typically spread on bread or toast.

TO YOUR HEALTH

Just as olive oil plays a key role in the healthful Mediterranean diet, so too can peanut butter be enjoyed as an integral part of a heart-healthy American diet. People who wish to eliminate or cut back on foods high in cholesterol and saturated fat may turn to peanut butter as a protein-rich ingredient in well-balanced meals. Most of the recipes in this book contain no meat or dairy products, thus making them accessible to almost everyone, including those who are vegan or lactose-intolerant. Both dairy and dairy-free options are provided in the ingredient lists.

Peanut butter adds creamy richness to recipes without the cholesterol and saturated fat of animal products. Some people may be surprised to discover that these recipes are so satisfying, they may never miss the meat. Since peanut butter is a good source of protein, it can be enjoyed as a meat alternative in a variety of globally inspired recipes. To me, as a vegan, this is one of the greatest benefits of this book.

For those who do eat meat, the editors have included suggestions following several recipes for ways to incorporate meat or seafood. Be advised, however, that making such additions to the recipes will significantly increase the calories and saturated fat content, as well as add cholesterol where none would otherwise exist. I would encourage anyone to first try these recipes in their original form and enjoy peanut butter in the same spirit in which Dr. Kellogg and others originally intended it to be eaten: as a delicious and satisfying meat alternative.

BUYING AND STORING TIPS

While many people enjoy the texture and convenience of regular peanut butter, which is almost universally available, others prefer 100 percent natural peanut butter because it has no stabilizers or other additives. All-natural peanut butter can be found in well-stocked supermarkets and natural food stores. Regular peanut butter may be stored on the pantry shelf, but all-natural peanut butter needs to be kept refrigerated to prevent rancidity.

When stored in a tightly sealed jar in the refrigerator, natural peanut butter will keep for several months. Because natural peanut butter is unprocessed, the oil and solids sometimes separate in the jar but can easily be stirred back together before use. Natural peanut butter also becomes stiff when chilled, so it is best to bring it to room temperature for a few minutes before use, to improve its spreadability.

ALLERGY ALTERNATIVES

It is estimated that 3 million Americans are allergic to peanuts. If you, or someone you cook for, are among them, talk to a doctor about substituting another nut butter for peanut butter. Among the delicious nut (and seed) butters you can make or buy are almond butter, cashew butter, pistachio butter, and sesame seed butter (also called tahini). Roasted soybeans are also made into a high-protein spread called soy nut butter. These nut butters can be used like peanut butter is used and are interchangeable in the recipes in this book.

Like peanut butter, other nut butters taste like an intense, creamy version of the nuts from which they were made. Unlike the economical peanut butter, however, most other nut butters can be quite expensive and are not as readily available as the ubiquitous peanut butter.

MORE THAN JUST A PB&J

Since our school lunch days, America's tastes have become more sophisticated. Not only are home cooks experimenting with ingredients and demanding greater variety in their daily meals, many are also cutting down on foods high in cholesterol and saturated fats. To fulfill those demands, many of the recipes in this book employ the healthful spread in exotic global cuisines, which have long included savory peanut butter dishes.

Whether in the spicy peanut sauces of Southeast Asia or the hearty stews of western Africa, irresistible peanut butter can be found in vibrant recipes from appetizers to main dishes. As the 80 sumptuous recipes in this book will attest, peanut butter has come of age. While it still makes a great sandwich, peanut butter is not just for kids anymore.

exotic peanut butter

For years, peanut butter has been used mainly for utilitarian sand-wiches—while sesame butter, or *tahini,* got all the attention as an exotic gourmet food item. Finally, peanut butter is getting the recog-nition it deserves, and America is discovering what the rest of the world has long known: Peanut butter can be used as a versatile main ingredient in sauces, main dishes, soups, dressings, and desserts—and can taste just as exotic as sesame butter.

homemade peanut butter

Peanut butter is easy to make at home from whole roasted peanuts using a high-speed blender or food processor. Grinding your own peanut butter can be a profoundly gratifying experience—not only is it easy and fun to make, but it also tastes great. Here's a recipe for homemade peanut butter. There's also a crunchy variation.

2 CUPS ROASTED SHELLED
PEANUTS

1 TABLESPOON PEANUT OIL

¼ TEASPOON SALT, OR TO TASTE
(OMIT IF SALTED PEANUTS ARE
USED)

1. Place the peanuts, oil, and salt, if using, in a food processor (or blender) and process (or blend) for 2 to 3 minutes. Stop to scrape down the sides with a rubber spatula and continue to process (or blend) until the desired consistency is reached.

2. Transfer to a tightly covered container and store in the refrigerator. For a more spreadable consistency, remove from the refrigerator about 20 minutes before using. If oil rises to the top, stir before using.

MAKES 1 CUP (1 TABLESPOON PER SERVING)

PER SERVING: 114 calories, 4 g protein, 4 g carbohydrates, 10 g total fat, 1 g saturated fat, 0 mg cholesterol, 1 g dietary fiber, 37 mg sodium

crunchy peanut butter

1 CUP HOMEMADE PEANUT BUTTER
(RECIPE ON OPPOSITE PAGE)

1/2 CUP CHOPPED ROASTED
PEANUTS

1. Place the peanut butter in a small bowl. Stir in the chopped roasted peanuts until blended.

2. Transfer to a tightly covered container and store in the refrigerator. For a more spreadable consistency, remove from the refrigerator about 20 minutes before using. If oil rises to the top, stir before using.

MAKES 1 1/2 CUPS (1 TABLESPOON PER SERVING)

PER SERVING: 92 calories, 4 g protein, 3 g carbohydrates, 8 g total fat, 1 g saturated fat, 0 mg cholesterol, 1 g dietary fiber, 25 mg sodium

soups

SOUTHERN PEANUT SOUP
12

CURRIED SWEET POTATO-PEANUT SOUP
14

PUMPKIN-PEANUT SOUP WITH PEANUT BUTTER CROUTONS
16

WEST AFRICAN PEANUT SOUP
18

PERUVIAN PEANUT-POTATO SOUP
19

INDONESIAN-INSPIRED COCONUT-PEANUT SOUP
20

CARROT-APPLE-PEANUT SOUP
22

southern peanut soup

Many cooks throughout the South have their own version of peanut soup. These soups all have one thing in common: the rich, creamy taste of peanut butter. If a thinner consistency is desired, stir in a little additional stock just before serving.

1 TABLESPOON OLIVE OIL

1 YELLOW ONION, CHOPPED

1 RIB CELERY, CHOPPED

1 LARGE BAKING POTATO, PEELED AND CHOPPED

5 CUPS VEGETABLE STOCK

3/4 CUP CREAMY PEANUT BUTTER

SALT AND FRESHLY GROUND BLACK PEPPER

1/4 CUP CHOPPED DRY-ROASTED PEANUTS

1. Heat the oil in a large pot over medium heat. Add the onion and celery, cover, and cook until softened, about 5 minutes. Add the potato and stock and bring to a boil. Reduce the heat to low and simmer uncovered until the vegetables are tender, about 30 minutes.

2. Remove the soup from the heat. Puree the mixture in a blender or food processor until smooth, or use an immersion blender to puree the soup right in the pot. Return all but 1 cup of the soup to the pot and return to a simmer.

3. Add the peanut butter to the reserved cup of soup and puree until smooth. Stir the peanut butter mixture into the soup, season to taste with salt and pepper, and simmer for 10 minutes to blend flavors.

4. To serve, ladle the soup into bowls and sprinkle with the chopped peanuts.

SERVES 6

PER SERVING: 360 calories, 12 g protein, 26 g carbohydrates, 25 g total fat, 4 g saturated fat, 0 mg cholesterol, 6 g dietary fiber, 470 mg sodium

peanut butter lowers risk of heart disease

According to the December 1999 issue of the *American Journal of Clinical Nutrition,* researchers at the Pennsylvania State University found that a diet rich in peanuts and peanut butter can reduce the risk of heart disease by 21 percent, compared to a 12 percent reduction from a traditional low-fat diet.

curried sweet potato–peanut soup (photo on page 10)

This soup has it all: great taste, vibrant color, and the creamy goodness of peanut butter. For a thinner soup, stir in a small amount of milk or soy milk during the final heating. I used Frontier brand organic curry powder, a heady blend of coriander, turmeric, cumin, mustard, fenugreek, cardamom, nutmeg, red pepper, cinnamon, and cloves for this recipe, but most any curry spice blend should perform well.

1 TABLESPOON PEANUT OIL

1 LARGE YELLOW ONION, CHOPPED

1 CLOVE GARLIC, CHOPPED

1 CAN (28 OUNCES) CRUSHED TOMATOES

5 CUPS VEGETABLE STOCK OR WATER

2 LARGE SWEET POTATOES, PEELED AND CUT INTO 1-INCH CHUNKS

¾ CUP CREAMY PEANUT BUTTER

1 TABLESPOON CURRY POWDER

¼ TEASPOON CAYENNE

SALT

¼ CUP CHOPPED DRY-ROASTED PEANUTS

1. Heat the oil in a large pot over medium heat. Add the onion and garlic, cover, and cook until softened, about 5 minutes.

2. Add the tomatoes, stock, and sweet potatoes. Bring to a boil, then reduce the heat to low and cook uncovered until the potatoes are soft, about 30 minutes.

3. Stir in the peanut butter, curry powder, cayenne, and salt to taste. Remove from the heat and allow to cool.

4. Puree the mixture in a blender or food processor until smooth, or use an immersion blender to puree the soup right in the pot. Heat the soup over low heat until hot. Serve sprinkled with the chopped peanuts.

SERVES 6

PER SERVING: 424 calories, 15 g protein, 39 g carbohydrates, 25 g total fat, 4 g saturated fat, 0 mg cholesterol, 9 g dietary fiber, 702 mg sodium

kid's corner: easiest peanut soup

Combine two parts vegetable stock with one part peanut butter in a saucepan, and simmer for 20 minutes. Season with salt and black pepper, to taste. Stir in a splash of milk or soy milk before serving, if desired.

pumpkin-peanut soup
with peanut butter croutons

A fresh pumpkin or orange-fleshed winter squash may be used instead of the canned pumpkin if desired. To do so, peel and seed the pumpkin or squash and cut it into ½-inch chunks. Add to the pot with the onion and proceed with the recipe. The hot chile may be omitted for those who prefer a mild soup.

SOUP:

1 TABLESPOON OLIVE OIL

1 LARGE YELLOW ONION, CHOPPED

1 CLOVE GARLIC, MINCED

½ RED OR YELLOW BELL PEPPER, CHOPPED

1 SMALL HOT CHILE, SEEDED AND MINCED (OPTIONAL)

1 CAN (14.5 OUNCES) DICED TOMATOES, UNDRAINED

1 CAN (16 OUNCES) SOLID-PACK PUMPKIN

4 CUPS VEGETABLE STOCK

¼ TEASPOON DRIED THYME

SALT AND FRESHLY GROUND BLACK PEPPER

¾ CUP CREAMY PEANUT BUTTER

CROUTONS:

2 TABLESPOONS CREAMY PEANUT BUTTER

2 TABLESPOONS OLIVE OIL

4 SLICES FIRM WHITE BREAD

FOR THE SOUP:

1. Heat the oil in a large pot over medium heat. Add the onion, garlic, bell pepper, and chile, if using. Cover and cook until softened, stirring occasionally, about 5 minutes.

2. Stir in the tomatoes, pumpkin, stock, thyme, and salt and pepper to taste. Bring to a boil, then reduce the heat to low, cover, and simmer for 45 minutes.

3. Stir in the peanut butter, then puree the mixture in a blender or food processor until smooth, or use an immersion blender to puree the soup right in the pot. Simmer the soup 10 to 15 minutes longer. Taste to adjust the seasonings.

FOR THE CROUTONS:

1. Preheat the oven to 400°F. Lightly oil a 10 × 15-inch baking pan and set aside.

2. In a small bowl, combine the peanut butter and oil, and blend until smooth.

3. Place a sheet of wax paper on a cutting board. Brush both sides of the bread slices with the peanut butter mixture and place on the wax paper. Cut each slice of bread lengthwise into $\frac{1}{2}$-inch strips, then cut the slices crosswise to form the croutons.

4. Separate the croutons and transfer them to the prepared pan. Bake until browned, stirring occasionally, about 8 minutes. Cool completely before using to garnish the soup. Store in an airtight container.

SERVES 6

PER SERVING: 516 calories, 15 g protein, 50 g carbohydrates, 31 g total fat, 4 g saturated fat, 0 mg cholesterol, 8 g dietary fiber, 811 mg sodium

west african peanut soup

Because peanuts are an abundant crop in Africa and a good, inexpensive source of protein, peanut soup can be found in many African countries. Traditionally, African peanut soups begin with whole peanuts that are ground to a paste, but beginning with peanut butter is infinitely more convenient.

1 TABLESPOON OLIVE OIL

1 LARGE YELLOW ONION, CHOPPED

1 LARGE RED BELL PEPPER, DICED

2 CLOVES GARLIC, CHOPPED

1 CAN (28 OUNCES) DICED TOMATOES, UNDRAINED

5 CUPS VEGETABLE STOCK

$1/2$ CUP BROWN RICE

$1/2$ TEASPOON CRUSHED RED-PEPPER FLAKES

SALT AND FRESHLY GROUND BLACK PEPPER

$3/4$ CUP CREAMY PEANUT BUTTER

2 TABLESPOONS CHOPPED DRY-ROASTED PEANUTS

1. Heat the oil in a large pot over medium heat. Add the onion, bell pepper, and garlic. Cover and cook until softened, about 5 minutes.

2. Stir in the tomatoes and their juice and the stock and bring to a boil. Add the rice, red-pepper flakes, and salt and pepper to taste. Reduce the heat to low and simmer, partially covered, until the rice is tender, about 40 minutes.

3. Ladle about 1 cup of soup into a small bowl, add the peanut butter, and stir until smooth. Stir the peanut butter mixture back into the soup until it is incorporated. Serve hot, sprinkled with the chopped peanuts.

SERVES 6

PER SERVING: 386 calories, 13 g protein, 35 g carbohydrates, 24 g total fat, 3 g saturated fat, 0 mg cholesterol, 6 g dietary fiber, 821 mg sodium

peruvian peanut-potato soup

The peanut plant is believed to have originated in South America. Records show that the Incas of Peru used peanuts as sacrificial offerings and entombed them with their mummies as early as 1500 BC. Since both peanuts and potatoes are Peruvian crops, they are combined in this flavorful soup. There are two ways to serve this soup. Served chunky, it is homey and rustic, and is especially good served with coarse dark bread. Puree the soup, and it turns a lovely butterscotch color and looks quite elegant, especially garnished with chives.

1 TABLESPOON OLIVE OIL

1 LARGE YELLOW ONION, CHOPPED

1 POUND ALL-PURPOSE POTATOES, PEELED AND DICED

6 CUPS VEGETABLE STOCK

$2/3$ CUP PEANUT BUTTER

SALT AND FRESHLY GROUND BLACK PEPPER

1 TABLESPOON CHOPPED CHIVES

1. Heat the oil in a large pot over medium heat. Add the onion, cover, and cook until softened, about 5 minutes. Add the potatoes and stock and cook until the potatoes are tender, about 40 minutes. Stir in the peanut butter and season with salt and pepper to taste.

2. If a chunky soup is desired, it can be served at this point, garnished with the chives. For a smooth soup, puree the mixture in a blender or food processor until smooth, or use an immersion blender to puree the soup right in the pot. Return the soup to the pot and heat over medium heat until hot, about 5 minutes. Serve garnished with the chives.

SERVES 6

PER SERVING: 307 calories, 10 g protein, 28 g carbohydrates, 19 g total fat, 3 g saturated fat, 0 mg cholesterol, 5 g dietary fiber, 374 mg sodium

indonesian-inspired coconut-peanut soup

The intense, vibrant flavors of Indonesia are the inspiration for this creamy soup redolent of ginger, lime juice, coconut, cilantro, and of course, peanut butter—all in a wonderful balance that is right on target. The bean sprouts add a nice crunch, while the cilantro adds a lovely color contrast to the pale orange soup. Blanch the bean sprouts for 30 seconds—just long enough to remove the raw taste.

1 TABLESPOON PEANUT OIL

3 SHALLOTS, CHOPPED

1 MEDIUM CARROT, CHOPPED

1 CLOVE GARLIC, CRUSHED

1 SMALL HOT CHILE, SEEDED AND MINCED (OPTIONAL)

1 TEASPOON MINCED FRESH GINGER

1 CAN (14.5 OUNCES) DICED TOMATOES, DRAINED

3 CUPS VEGETABLE STOCK

1 TEASPOON FRESH LIME JUICE

1 TEASPOON LIGHT BROWN SUGAR

$1/4$ TEASPOON CAYENNE

SALT AND FRESHLY GROUND BLACK PEPPER

$3/4$ CUP PEANUT BUTTER

1 CUP UNSWEETENED COCONUT MILK

$1/2$ CUP FRESH BEAN SPROUTS, BLANCHED

2 TABLESPOONS MINCED FRESH CILANTRO LEAVES

1. Heat the oil in a large pot over medium heat. Add the shallots and carrot, cover, and cook until softened, about 5 minutes.

2. Add the garlic, chile (if using), ginger, tomatoes, stock, lime juice, sugar, cayenne, and salt and pepper to taste. Bring to a boil, then reduce the heat to low and simmer until the vegetables are tender, about 20 minutes. Stir in the peanut butter and remove from the heat.

3. Puree the mixture in a blender or food processor until smooth, or use an immersion blender to puree the soup right in the pot. Return to the pot, stir in the coconut milk, and simmer until hot. Serve garnished with bean sprouts and cilantro.

SERVES 6

PER SERVING: 385 calories, 12 g protein, 20 g carbohydrates, 32 g total fat, 12 g saturated fat, 0 mg cholesterol, 5 g dietary fiber, 480 mg sodium

variation: Cooked shrimp may be added to the soup when ready to serve.

carrot-apple-peanut soup

This bright and versatile soup can be served piping hot in cold weather, but it's also re-freshingly delicious when served cold. I like to use a tart Granny Smith apple, but a sweeter variety such as Fuji or Gala may be used.

1 TABLESPOON PEANUT OIL

1 YELLOW ONION, DICED

1 POUND CARROTS, PEELED AND CHOPPED

1 RIB CELERY, CHOPPED

1 BAKING POTATO, PEELED AND CHOPPED

1 LARGE COOKING APPLE, PEELED, CUT IN CHUNKS

2 TEASPOONS MINCED FRESH GINGER

1/4 TEASPOON CINNAMON

3 CUPS VEGETABLE STOCK OR WATER

1 CUP APPLE JUICE

SALT AND FRESHLY GROUND BLACK PEPPER

1/2 CUP CREAMY PEANUT BUTTER

1 SMALL APPLE, UNPEELED, THINLY SLICED

2 TABLESPOONS CHOPPED DRY-ROASTED PEANUTS

1. Heat the oil in a large pot over medium heat. Add the onion, carrots, celery, and potato. Cover and cook for 5 minutes, stirring occasionally, until the vegetables are softened. Add the large apple, ginger, cinnamon, stock, apple juice, and salt and pepper to taste. Cover and bring to a boil. Reduce the heat and simmer until the vegetables are tender, 20 to 30 minutes. Stir in the peanut butter.

2. Puree the mixture in a blender or food processor until smooth, or use an immersion blender to puree the soup right in the pot. Pour the soup back into the pot and heat until hot. (If serving cold, pour the soup into a container and refrigerate until chilled.) Serve garnished with apple slices and chopped peanuts.

SERVES 6

PER SERVING: 316 calories, 9 g protein, 36 g carbohydrates, 17 g total fat, 2 g saturated fat, 0 mg cholesterol, 7 g dietary fiber, 334 mg sodium

starters

ASIAN SPRING ROLLS WITH SPICY PEANUT DIPPING SAUCE
26

PEANUT BUTTER HUMMUS
28

SAVORY THREE-NUT PÂTÉ
29

VEGETABLE TEMPURA WITH PEANUT-SOY DIPPING SAUCE
30

FIRE ANTS ON A LOG
32

SPICY SPINACH-PEANUT CROSTINI
33

WONTON CRISPS WITH THAI PEANUT SPREAD
34

CRUDITÉS WITH SPICY PEANUT DIP
36

SPICE-RUBBED VEGETABLE SATAYS WITH PEANUT SAUCE
38

BELGIAN ENDIVE WITH PEANUT-PINEAPPLE CREAM CHEESE
40

PEANUT BUTTER AND PEPPER JELLY PINWHEELS
41

asian spring rolls with spicy peanut dipping sauce

Spring roll wrappers, made of fragile rice paper, are brittle when you buy them, but soften easily when soaked in water. They are available in Asian markets.

SAUCE:

1/4 CUP CREAMY PEANUT BUTTER

2 TABLESPOONS TAMARI OR OTHER SOY SAUCE

1/3 CUP WATER

1 TABLESPOON RICE VINEGAR

1 TABLESPOON FRESH LIME JUICE

1 TEASPOON FINELY MINCED GARLIC

1 TEASPOON LIGHT BROWN SUGAR

1/4 TEASPOON CRUSHED RED-PEPPER FLAKES, OR TO TASTE

1 TABLESPOON MINCED CILANTRO LEAVES

SPRING ROLLS:

8 SPRING ROLL WRAPPERS

8 BOSTON LETTUCE LEAVES OR OTHER SOFT LEAF LETTUCE

1 1/2 CUPS SHREDDED CARROTS

1 CUP FRESH BEAN SPROUTS

1/2 CUP CHOPPED CILANTRO

1. In a small bowl or food processor, combine the peanut butter, tamari, water, vinegar, lime juice, garlic, sugar, and red-pepper flakes until well blended. Taste to adjust the seasonings. Add more water if the sauce is too thick.

2. Set aside while you make the spring rolls, or cover and refrigerate until ready to use. Add minced cilantro to the sauce just prior to serving time.

FOR THE SPRING ROLLS:

1. Dip a wrapper into a shallow bowl of warm water just long enough to soften. Remove the wrapper from the water and place on a piece of plastic wrap on a flat work surface. Place a lettuce leaf on top of the wrapper and arrange a small amount of the carrots, sprouts, and chopped cilantro on the bottom third of the lettuce leaf. Bring the bottom edge of the wrapper over the filling and fold in the sides tightly. Use your finger to spread water along the top edge and roll tightly, using the plastic wrap to help roll it up.

2. Place the roll seam side down on a serving platter. Repeat with the remaining wrappers, lettuce, and filling ingredients. When assembly is finished, serve the rolls with the peanut sauce for dipping.

SERVES 4

PER SERVING: 281 calories, 12 g protein, 39 g carbohydrates, 11 g total fat, 1 g saturated fat, 0 mg cholesterol, 4 g dietary fiber, 780 mg sodium

variation: Optional filling ingredients may include cooked thin rice noodles, baked tofu strips, minced scallion, cooked shrimp, or cooked strips of chicken.

peanut butter hummus

Peanut butter stands in for the traditional sesame paste in this flavorful, protein-rich dip.

1½ CUPS COOKED CHICKPEAS OR ONE 15-OUNCE CAN CHICKPEAS, DRAINED AND RINSED

¼ CUP PEANUT BUTTER

3 TABLESPOONS FRESH LEMON JUICE

1 LARGE CLOVE GARLIC, CHOPPED

1 TABLESPOON MINCED PARSLEY

½ TEASPOON SALT

1. Puree the chickpeas in a food processor. Add the peanut butter, lemon juice, garlic, parsley, and salt. Process until smooth and well blended. Add some water if a thinner consistency is desired.

2. Transfer to a tightly covered container and refrigerate for at least an hour before serving to allow flavors to develop. Serve chilled or at room temperature.

MAKES ABOUT 2 CUPS (2 TABLESPOONS PER SERVING)

PER SERVING: 55 calories, 2 g protein, 6 g carbohydrates, 3 g total fat, 0 g saturated fat, 0 mg cholesterol, 2 g dietary fiber, 83 mg sodium

savory three-nut pâté

This lovely pâté can be garnished with ground nuts and fresh herbs. Chill and serve whole or sliced on a buffet table with an assortment of crackers and breads, or serve it warm as a delicious dinner entrée. It also makes a great cold snack right out of the fridge.

1 TABLESPOON OLIVE OIL

1 LARGE YELLOW ONION, MINCED

1 CLOVE GARLIC, MINCED

3/4 CUP PEANUT BUTTER

1 1/2 TABLESPOONS BRANDY OR FRANGELICO (OPTIONAL)

3/4 TEASPOON DRIED THYME

1/2 TEASPOON SALT

1/8 TEASPOON CAYENNE

2 CUPS WALNUT PIECES

1 CUP BLANCHED ALMONDS

2 TABLESPOONS CHOPPED FRESH PARSLEY

2 TABLESPOONS ALL-PURPOSE FLOUR

1. Lightly oil a 6-cup loaf pan or pâté mold. Preheat the oven to 350°F.

2. Heat the oil in a large skillet over medium heat. Add the onion and garlic. Cover and cook until softened, about 5 minutes. Add the peanut butter, brandy (if using), thyme, salt, and cayenne and stir to blend for 1 to 2 minutes. Set aside.

3. Place the walnuts and almonds in a food processor and pulse until coarsely chopped. Add the parsley and flour and pulse to combine. Add the reserved peanut butter mixture and process until just combined, leaving some texture. Taste to adjust the seasonings, then spoon into the prepared pan. Bake until firm, about 45 minutes.

4. Let the pâté cool at room temperature, then refrigerate it until chilled completely for easier slicing. When ready to serve, remove the pâté from the mold, or run a knife along the edge of the loaf pan and invert onto a plate.

SERVES 12

PER SERVING: 338 calories, 10 g protein, 12 g carbohydrates, 30 g total fat, 3 g saturated fat, 0 mg cholesterol, 5 g dietary fiber, 139 mg sodium

vegetable tempura with peanut-soy dipping sauce

Use thinly sliced vegetables so they cook quickly, and deep-fry them in small batches, maintaining a temperature of 350°F. When you add the flour, whisk quickly and just enough to mix it in evenly.

SAUCE:

1/4 CUP TAMARI OR OTHER SOY SAUCE

1/4 CUP WATER

2 TABLESPOONS FRESH LEMON JUICE

2 TABLESPOONS PEANUT BUTTER

2 TEASPOONS LIGHT BROWN SUGAR

1 TEASPOON GRATED FRESH GINGER

1 SCALLION, FINELY MINCED

TEMPURA:

1 EGG YOLK OR 1 TABLESPOON BLENDED EGG SUBSTITUTE

1 CUP VERY COLD WATER, OR MORE

2 TABLESPOONS SAKE OR DRY WHITE WINE (OPTIONAL)

1 CUP ALL-PURPOSE FLOUR

PEANUT OIL

1 POUND ASSORTED SLICED VEGETABLES, PATTED DRY (GOOD CHOICES INCLUDE CARROT, ONION, BELL PEPPER, ZUCCHINI, BUTTERNUT SQUASH, SWEET POTATO, BROCCOLI, AND MUSHROOMS)

FOR THE SAUCE:

1. In a blender or food processor, combine the tamari, water, lemon juice, peanut butter, and sugar. Blend until smooth.

2. Pour into dipping bowls. Top with the ginger and scallion.

FOR THE TEMPURA:

1. Combine the egg yolk, water, and sake (if using) in a bowl. Add the flour and mix until just combined. Do not overmix. The batter should be lumpy. If the batter is too thick, thin it with a little more water.

2. Heat about 4 inches of peanut oil in a saucepan or a deep-fat fryer to 350°F. Working in batches, dip the vegetables into the batter and shake off the excess. Fry until crisp and golden, turning the vegetables occasionally to cook evenly, about 3 minutes. Remove with a slotted spoon to a baking pan lined with paper towels to drain. Serve immediately with the dipping sauce.

SERVES 4

PER SERVING: 250 calories, 10 g protein, 42 g carbohydrates, 5 g total fat, 1 g saturated fat, 0 mg cholesterol, 5 g dietary fiber, 1,264 mg sodium

variation: Large peeled and deveined shrimp can also be dipped in the tempura batter and cooked for 2 to 3 minutes in addition to the vegetables.

fire ants on a log

This is a grown-up version of that kindergarten favorite, with a spicy heat that is suited to adult tastes. This recipe can be adjusted for a solo snack or to feed a crowd. If the red color of the cranberries provides enough "fire" for you, you can eliminate the spicy-hot "fire" of the cayenne.

5 OR 6 RIBS CELERY

½ CUP SMOOTH OR CRUNCHY PEANUT BUTTER

1 TEASPOON MAPLE SYRUP

¼ TEASPOON CAYENNE, OR TO TASTE

½ CUP SWEETENED DRIED CRANBERRIES

1. Trim the ends from the celery and, using a vegetable peeler or sharp paring knife, remove a thin strip lengthwise from along the curved back of each celery rib so they sit flat without wobbling. Set aside.

2. In a bowl, combine the peanut butter, maple syrup, and cayenne, stirring to blend.

3. Stuff the peanut butter mixture into the celery pieces and gently press the cranberries into the peanut butter. To serve as a finger food, cut the celery into bite-size pieces (about 1 inch long) and arrange on a platter. Otherwise, they may be cut in half or left whole.

SERVES 4

PER SERVING: 292 calories, 9 g protein, 25 g carbohydrates, 20 g total fat, 3 g saturated fat, 0 mg cholesterol, 5 g dietary fiber, 138 mg sodium

spicy spinach-peanut crostini (photo on page 24)

This popular Italian appetizer is made with toasted bread rounds that are usually rubbed with a cut clove of garlic and crowned with a savory topping.

1 PACKAGE (10 OUNCES) FROZEN CHOPPED SPINACH, THAWED

1 TABLESPOON PLUS ¼ CUP OLIVE OIL

1 CLOVE GARLIC, FINELY MINCED

2 TABLESPOONS PEANUT BUTTER

½ TEASPOON CRUSHED RED-PEPPER FLAKES

SALT

1 BAGUETTE, CUT INTO ½-INCH-THICK SLICES

1 LARGE CLOVE GARLIC, HALVED

1 TABLESPOON CHOPPED ROASTED PEANUTS

1. Cook the spinach according to package directions. Drain well, squeezing out all of the water.

2. Heat 1 tablespoon olive oil in a medium skillet over medium heat. Add the minced garlic and cook until fragrant, about 30 seconds. Stir in the spinach, peanut butter, red-pepper flakes, and salt to taste, blending the peanut butter into the spinach.

3. Preheat the oven to 400°F. Pour the ¼ cup olive oil into a shallow bowl and dip each slice of bread in it to coat one side. Place the bread oiled side up on a baking sheet and bake until golden brown, about 10 minutes. When the bread is toasted, remove it from the oven and rub the oiled side with the cut sides of the halved garlic clove.

4. Top each piece of bread with a small amount of the spinach topping. Sprinkle with chopped peanuts and serve hot.

SERVES 6

PER SERVING: 294 calories, 5 g protein, 14 g carbohydrates, 25 g total fat, 3 g saturated fat, 0 mg cholesterol, 2 g dietary fiber, 154 mg sodium

wonton crisps with thai peanut spread

Wonton wrappers are available in the refrigerated case (usually in the produce section) of well-stocked supermarkets. If unavailable, use thin slices of toasted French bread. Use two or more of the topping suggestions on each crisp for a taste and textural contrast. For example, try the shredded cucumber and carrots with chopped dry-roasted peanuts or toasted coconut.

12 WONTON WRAPPERS

PEANUT OIL OR OTHER LIGHT FLAVORLESS OIL

1/2 CUP CRUNCHY PEANUT BUTTER

1/3 CUP COCONUT MILK

2 TABLESPOONS FRESH LIME JUICE

2 TEASPOONS TAMARI OR OTHER SOY SAUCE

1 TEASPOON LIGHT BROWN SUGAR

1/2 TEASPOON CRUSHED RED-PEPPER FLAKES, OR TO TASTE

TOPPINGS:

SHREDDED GREEN PAPAYA, TOASTED COCONUT, SHREDDED CUCUMBER, SHREDDED CARROT, CHOPPED DRY-ROASTED PEANUTS, MINCED CRYSTALLIZED GINGER

1. Preheat the oven to 350°F. Cut the wonton wrappers diagonally to make 24 triangles. Lightly brush both sides of the wrappers with a small amount of peanut oil. Arrange on baking sheets and bake until crisp, 5 to 7 minutes. Remove from the oven and set aside to cool.

2. In a bowl, combine the peanut butter, coconut milk, lime juice, tamari, sugar, and red-pepper flakes until well blended. Spread a thin coating of the peanut mixture on each wonton, sprinkle on a small amount of the desired toppings, and serve at once.

SERVES 4

PER SERVING: 297 calories, 10 g protein, 22 g carbohydrates, 20 g total fat, 6 g saturated fat, 2 mg cholesterol, 3 g dietary fiber, 421 mg sodium

variation: Toppings could also include minced cooked shrimp or shredded crabmeat.

that's a lot of jars

The amount of peanut butter eaten in a year could wrap the earth in a

ribbon of 18-ounce peanut butter jars one and one-third times.

crudités with spicy peanut dip

Choose your favorite assortment of vegetables, cut into sticks, slices, or other appropriate shapes. Arrange them on a platter, add the dip, and you have a party!

DIP:

1/4 CUP PEANUT BUTTER

1/4 CUP PEACH OR APRICOT JAM

1 TEASPOON GRATED FRESH GINGER

1/2 TEASPOON MINCED GARLIC

1 TABLESPOON FRESH LIME JUICE

1 TABLESPOON TAMARI OR OTHER SOY SAUCE

1/8 TEASPOON CAYENNE, OR TO TASTE

VEGETABLES:

2 LARGE CARROTS, PEELED AND CUT INTO 1/4 × 4-INCH STICKS

2 OUNCES SNOW PEAS, ENDS TRIMMED AND TOUGH STRING REMOVED

3 RIBS CELERY, TRIMMED AND CUT INTO 1/4 × 4-INCH STICKS

1 LARGE RED OR YELLOW BELL PEPPER, SEEDED AND CUT INTO 1/4-INCH STRIPS

1 HEAD BELGIAN ENDIVE, TRIMMED

FOR THE DIP:

1. Combine the peanut butter, jam, gingerroot, garlic, lime juice, tamari, and cayenne in a small bowl. Stir until thoroughly blended. A small amount of water may be added if a thinner consistency is desired.

2. Transfer the dip to a small serving bowl and place it in the center of a serving tray or platter.

FOR THE VEGETABLES:

1. Arrange all the vegetables on the serving tray in a decorative fashion, surrounding the bowl of dip.

2. Serve at once or cover and refrigerate until ready to serve.

SERVES 6

PER SERVING: 160 calories, 6 g protein, 22 g carbohydrates, 7 g total fat, 1 g saturated fat, 0 mg cholesterol, 6 g dietary fiber, 248 mg sodium

psych department

Did you know there is an actual name for the fear of getting peanut

butter stuck to the roof of your mouth? It's called arachibutyrophobia.

Now, *that's* a mouthful!

spice-rubbed vegetable satays with peanut sauce

These tasty skewered vegetables are a crowd pleaser whether plated individually or heaped on a platter and served on a buffet. Be sure to soak bamboo skewers in cold water for 30 minutes to prevent them from burning.

³/₄ CUP UNSWEETENED COCONUT MILK

2 TABLESPOONS PEANUT BUTTER

1 TABLESPOON MINCED FRESH GINGER

1 CLOVE GARLIC, MINCED

1 TABLESPOON LIGHT BROWN SUGAR

1 TABLESPOON TAMARI OR OTHER SOY SAUCE

1 TABLESPOON FRESH LEMON JUICE

¹/₄ TEASPOON CHILI POWDER

¹/₄ TEASPOON ALLSPICE

¹/₄ TEASPOON SUGAR

¹/₄ TEASPOON SALT

¹/₄ TEASPOON CAYENNE

1 EGGPLANT, HALVED LENGTHWISE AND CUT CROSSWISE INTO ¹/₄-INCH SLICES

1 LARGE RED BELL PEPPER, HALVED LENGTHWISE, SEEDED, AND CUT INTO 1-INCH STRIPS

2 PORTOBELLO MUSHROOM CAPS, CUT INTO ¹/₄-INCH SLICES

2 TABLESPOONS TOASTED SESAME OIL

4 LEAVES LEAF LETTUCE

6 ORANGE SLICES, HALVED

1. In a bowl or food processor, combine the coconut milk, peanut butter, ginger, garlic, brown sugar, tamari, and lemon juice. Blend until smooth. Transfer to a saucepan and simmer on low heat until slightly thickened, stirring frequently, about 10 minutes. Set aside.

2. In a small bowl, combine the chili powder, allspice, sugar, salt, and cayenne. Set aside.

3. Preheat the broiler or grill. Place the eggplant, bell pepper, and mushroom slices in a large bowl and drizzle with the oil. Toss to coat. Sprinkle the vegetables with the reserved spice mixture, tossing to coat. Press any remaining spice mixture from the bottom of the bowl into the vegetables so the spices adhere.

4. Thread the vegetables onto skewers and place them under the broiler or on the grill until well browned, about 3 minutes per side.

5. Arrange the satays on plates lined with lettuce leaves. Divide the reserved peanut sauce among 4 small dipping bowls and place them on the plates with the satays. Garnish with 3 orange slices each and serve at once.

SERVES 4

PER SERVING: 296 calories, 7 g protein, 22 g carbohydrates, 23 g total fat, 11 g saturated fat, 0 mg cholesterol, 9 g dietary fiber, 411 mg sodium

variation: Thinly sliced chicken or pork may be threaded onto the skewers instead of the vegetables. They will cook in approximately the same amount of time as the vegetables. The versatile and delicious satay sauce can also be used to top grilled shrimp or fish.

belgian endive with peanut-pineapple cream cheese

This yummy appetizer tastes like dessert and looks especially appealing on a tray when the leaves are arranged to resemble a flower.

1 CAN (8 OUNCES) CRUSHED PINEAPPLE, WELL DRAINED AND BLOTTED

1 PACKAGE (8 OUNCES) REGULAR, LOW-FAT, OR TOFU CREAM CHEESE, SOFTENED

1/2 CUP PEANUT BUTTER

2 HEADS BELGIAN ENDIVE

1/2 CUP FINELY CRUSHED DRY-ROASTED PEANUTS

CURLY ENDIVE (CHICORY)

1. In a medium bowl, combine the pineapple, cream cheese, and peanut butter. Blend well and set aside.

2. Trim the stem ends off the endive and separate the individual leaves.

3. Use a pastry bag, a zip-top bag, or a spoon to distribute about 2 teaspoons of the peanut butter filling into the bottom of each leaf. Sprinkle the filling with the crushed peanuts. Arrange the filled leaves on a round plate in a spokelike fashion to resemble a flower, with some curly endive leaves placed in the center of the plate for garnish.

MAKES ABOUT 24

PER STUFFED ENDIVE LEAF: 99 calories, 3 g protein, 5 g carbohydrates, 8 g total fat, 3 g saturated fat, 10 mg cholesterol, 2 g dietary fiber, 50 mg sodium

peanut butter and pepper jelly pinwheels

Brimming with color, texture, and flavor, this no-cook appetizer is easy to assemble on a moment's notice.

½ CUP CRUNCHY PEANUT BUTTER

2 TABLESPOONS REGULAR OR SOY MAYONNAISE

¼ CUP FINELY MINCED CELERY

2 TABLESPOONS FINELY MINCED PITTED BLACK OLIVES

½ CUP HOT OR MILD PEPPER JELLY

1 LARGE CARROT, GRATED

2 PIECES LAVASH FLATBREAD OR FLOUR TORTILLAS

1. In a small bowl, combine the peanut butter, mayonnaise, celery, and olives. Mix well and set aside.

2. In a separate bowl, combine the pepper jelly and grated carrot and set aside.

3. Place one piece of the lavash on a cutting board and spread evenly with half of the peanut butter mixture. Spread half of the jelly mixture on top. Roll up the bread and use a serrated knife to cut the roll into 1-inch pieces. Stand the pieces upright on a platter and repeat with the remaining ingredients.

SERVES 4

PER SERVING: 376 calories, 8 g protein, 40 g carbohydrates, 23 g total fat, 3 g saturated fat, 3 mg cholesterol, 4 g dietary fiber, 222 mg sodium

note: Soft white bread with the crusts removed may be used instead of the lavash or tortillas, if desired.

salads

COLD NOODLE SALAD WITH SPICY PEANUT SAUCE
44

CRUNCHY COLESLAW WITH CREAMY PEANUT DRESSING
45

MIXED BABY GREENS AND GREEN PAPAYA
WITH THAI PEANUT DRESSING
46

INDONESIAN GADO-GADO
48

PEANUT LOVER'S POTATO SALAD
50

SWEET POTATO SALAD
51

WALDORF SALAD REDUX
52

TROPICAL FRUIT SALAD WITH PEANUT-RUM DRESSING
53

cold noodle salad with spicy peanut sauce

This satisfying salad makes a great make-ahead meal. The hint of sesame oil complements the peanut butter nicely. Linguine noodles are used because they are sturdy and easy to find, but if you prefer, substitute Asian noodles.

½ CUP CREAMY PEANUT BUTTER

4 TEASPOONS TAMARI OR OTHER SOY SAUCE

2 TABLESPOONS RICE WINE VINEGAR

¼ TEASPOON CAYENNE, OR TO TASTE

2 CLOVES GARLIC, MINCED

1 TEASPOON MINCED FRESH GINGER

½ CUP WATER

12 OUNCES LINGUINE

1 TABLESPOON TOASTED SESAME OIL

1 LARGE CARROT, SHREDDED

1 RED BELL PEPPER, CUT INTO MATCHSTICK JULIENNE STRIPS

3 SCALLIONS, THINLY SLICED

1. In a medium bowl, combine the peanut butter, tamari, vinegar, cayenne, garlic, and ginger, stirring to blend well. Add the water (up to ½ cup) to make a thick sauce. Set aside.

2. Cook the linguine in a large pot of boiling water until al dente, 8 to 10 minutes. Drain and rinse the linguine under cold water and transfer to a large bowl. Toss with the sesame oil to coat.

3. Add the carrot, bell pepper, and scallions to the bowl with the linguine. Add the reserved peanut sauce to coat, tossing gently to combine. Refrigerate for 30 minutes before serving.

SERVES 6

PER SERVING: 398 calories, 15 g protein, 51 g carbohydrates, 17 g total fat, 2 g saturated fat, 0 mg cholesterol, 5 g dietary fiber, 525 mg sodium

variation: Cooked shrimp or strips of cooked chicken may be added to this dish when combining the vegetables, noodles, and sauce.

crunchy coleslaw with creamy peanut dressing

The addition of cilantro gives this slaw an exotic Southeast Asian flavor, which can be further amplified by replacing the lemon juice with lime juice and adding a dash of red-pepper flakes. For a more mainstream slaw, use the parsley instead of cilantro. Either way, the peanut butter adds a new and flavorful twist to the popular cabbage salad.

4 CUPS SHREDDED GREEN CABBAGE

1 LARGE CARROT, GRATED

2 TABLESPOONS MINCED CILANTRO OR PARSLEY

1/4 CUP PEANUT BUTTER

1/4 CUP MAYONNAISE OR SOY MAYONNAISE

2 TABLESPOONS FRESH LEMON JUICE

1 TABLESPOON WHITE WINE VINEGAR

1 TEASPOON SUGAR

SALT AND FRESHLY GROUND BLACK PEPPER

1. In a large bowl, combine the cabbage, carrot, and cilantro. Set aside.

2. In a small bowl, combine the peanut butter, mayonnaise, lemon juice, vinegar, sugar, and salt and pepper to taste. Stir until well blended.

3. Pour the dressing over the vegetables and toss gently to coat. Taste and adjust seasoning. Refrigerate, covered, until ready to serve.

SERVES 4

PER SERVING: 251 calories, 6 g protein, 13 g carbohydrates, 21 g total fat, 3 g saturated fat, 5 mg cholesterol, 4 g dietary fiber, 140 mg sodium

mixed baby greens and green papaya with thai peanut dressing (photo on page x)

This refreshing Thai-inspired salad is spicy, sweet, and crunchy. Green papayas are available in Asian markets. The easiest way to shred them is with a mandoline or other slicer, like the Benriner.

2 TABLESPOONS PEANUT BUTTER

1 LARGE CLOVE GARLIC, FINELY MINCED

1 TEASPOON MINCED FRESH GINGER

1/2 TEASPOON CRUSHED RED-PEPPER FLAKES, OR TO TASTE

1 TABLESPOON LIGHT BROWN SUGAR

1/4 CUP FRESH LIME JUICE

2 TABLESPOONS TAMARI OR OTHER SOY SAUCE

1 GREEN PAPAYA, PEELED, HALVED LENGTHWISE, AND SEEDED

1 SMALL CARROT

4 CUPS MIXED BABY GREENS

1/3 CUP CHOPPED ROASTED PEANUTS

1. In a small bowl, combine the peanut butter, garlic, ginger, red-pepper flakes, and sugar. Blend in the lime juice and tamari and set aside.

2. Shred the papaya using a mandoline. If you don't have a mandoline-type slicer, use a box grater, a food processor with a shredding disk, or a sharp knife. Place the shredded papaya in a large bowl. Shred the carrot in the same way, place in a small bowl, and set aside.

3. Pour about one-third of the reserved dressing over the papaya and toss to combine. Set aside.

4. Toss the greens with the remaining dressing and arrange on 4 salad plates. Top each salad with a portion of the reserved papaya and sprinkle each with the chopped peanuts and reserved carrot.

SERVES 4

PER SERVING: 180 calories, 7 g protein, 17 g carbohydrates, 11 g total fat, 2 g saturated fat, 0 mg cholesterol, 5 g dietary fiber, 506 mg sodium

variation: This salad may be topped with cooked shrimp or thinly sliced cooked beef or chicken.

all in a day's work

The world's largest peanut butter factory churns out 250,000 jars of the tasty spread daily.

indonesian gado-gado

Gado-Gado is an Indonesian main-dish salad composed of raw and cooked vegetables tossed with a spicy peanut sauce. The flavor improves with time, so plan on making this crunchy salad the day before you need it.

1 TABLESPOON PEANUT OIL

2 SHALLOTS, CHOPPED

1 LARGE CLOVE GARLIC, CHOPPED

½ CUP PEANUT BUTTER

1½ TABLESPOONS TAMARI OR OTHER SOY SAUCE

1½ TABLESPOONS FRESH LEMON JUICE

1 TEASPOON LIGHT BROWN SUGAR

¼ TEASPOON CAYENNE

¾ CUP UNSWEETENED COCONUT MILK

2 CUPS GREEN BEANS, CUT INTO 1-INCH LENGTHS

1 CUP SMALL CAULIFLOWER FLORETS

2 CARROTS, SHREDDED

2 CUPS SHREDDED CABBAGE

1 CUP FRESH BEAN SPROUTS

⅓ CUP ROASTED PEANUTS

1. Heat the oil in a skillet over medium heat. Add the shallots and garlic. Cover and cook until softened, about 5 minutes. Stir in the peanut butter, tamari, lemon juice, sugar, cayenne, and coconut milk. Simmer over low heat for 2 minutes, stirring to blend.

2. Transfer the mixture to a blender or food processor, or use an immersion blender, and puree until smooth, adding water or more coconut milk to thin, if needed.

3. Steam the green beans and cauliflower just until tender and place them in a large bowl. Add the carrots and cabbage. Pour the sauce over the vegetables and toss to combine. Sprinkle the bean sprouts and peanuts on top. Cover and refrigerate until ready to serve.

SERVES 6

PER SERVING: 333 calories, 11 g protein, 19 g carbohydrates, 26 g total fat, 9 g saturated fat, 0 mg cholesterol, 6 g dietary fiber, 308 mg sodium

circle the calendar

The month of November is designated as Peanut Butter Lovers' Month. Why not celebrate with an "everything peanut butter" potluck? Ask fellow peanut butter lovers to prepare dishes containing peanut butter and share them at a celebratory potluck dinner to honor the noble spread. (Hint: Assign each participant a category such as Appetizer, Main Course, Salad, or Dessert—otherwise you may get 10 trays of peanut butter and jelly sandwiches!)

peanut lover's potato salad

This hearty salad, with its rich peanutty undertones, is also delicious served warm. For a lovely color accent, stir in some thawed frozen green peas.

1½ POUNDS SMALL RED-SKINNED POTATOES, HALVED OR QUARTERED

1 SMALL RIB CELERY, MINCED

2 TABLESPOONS GRATED ONION

⅓ CUP DRY-ROASTED PEANUTS

½ CUP REGULAR OR SOY MAYONNAISE

¼ CUP PEANUT BUTTER

2 TABLESPOONS MINCED PARSLEY

SALT AND FRESHLY GROUND BLACK PEPPER

1. Steam the potatoes over boiling water until tender but still firm, 15 to 20 minutes. Drain and place in a large bowl. Add the celery, onion, and peanuts, and set aside.

2. In a small bowl, combine the mayonnaise, peanut butter, parsley, and salt and pepper to taste. Mix well and add to the potato mixture, stirring gently to combine. Serve right away or cover and refrigerate until ready to serve.

SERVES 6

PER SERVING: 338 calories, 7 g protein, 23 g carbohydrates, 25 g total fat, 3 g saturated fat, 7 mg cholesterol, 4 g dietary fiber, 139 mg sodium

sweet potato salad

This colorful dish is both a nice change from traditional potato salad and an unusual way to serve sweet potatoes.

1½ POUNDS SWEET POTATOES

1 TABLESPOON OLIVE OIL

1 CUP FROZEN BABY PEAS, THAWED

2 SCALLIONS, MINCED

½ CUP PINEAPPLE OR ORANGE JUICE

¼ CUP PEANUT BUTTER

SALT AND FRESHLY GROUND BLACK PEPPER

2 TABLESPOONS CHOPPED DRY-ROASTED PEANUTS

1. Preheat the oven to 400°F. Peel the potatoes and cut them into ½-inch dice. Toss with the olive oil and spread on a baking sheet. Roast the potatoes until tender but still firm, about 30 minutes. Allow to cool, then place in a large bowl. Add the peas and scallions and set aside.

2. In a small bowl, combine the juice, peanut butter, and salt and pepper to taste. Blend well, then pour the dressing over the potato mixture, stirring gently to combine. Sprinkle with chopped peanuts and serve right away, or cover and refrigerate until ready to serve.

SERVES 4

PER SERVING: 397 calories, 11 g protein, 60 g carbohydrates, 16 g total fat, 2 g saturated fat, 0 mg cholesterol, 10 g dietary fiber, 160 mg sodium

waldorf salad redux

This decidedly nontraditional Waldorf salad pairs peanut butter and dried cranberries alongside the traditional apples and celery, making this dish an especially pretty addition to a holiday dinner table. I like to use sweet Red Delicious apples with the peels left on for added color and crunch. Be sure to wash the apples really well.

4 RED DELICIOUS APPLES, CORED

1 TABLESPOON FRESH LEMON JUICE

1 CUP FINELY MINCED CELERY

¾ CUP COARSELY CHOPPED DRY-ROASTED PEANUTS

⅓ CUP SWEETENED DRIED CRANBERRIES

1 SCALLION, FINELY MINCED (OPTIONAL)

⅓ CUP REGULAR OR SOY MAYONNAISE

¼ CUP PEANUT BUTTER

¼ TEASPOON SUGAR

¼ TEASPOON SALT

1. Cut the apples into ½-inch dice and place them in a large bowl. Add the lemon juice and toss to coat. Add the celery, ½ cup of the peanuts, cranberries, and scallion (if using), and set aside.

2. In a small bowl, combine the mayonnaise, peanut butter, sugar, and salt, stirring to blend. Add the sauce to the apple mixture and stir gently to combine. Taste to adjust the seasonings.

3. Sprinkle with the remaining ¼ cup peanuts and serve at once, or cover and refrigerate until ready to use. This salad is best if served on the same day it is made.

SERVES 6

PER SERVING: 349 calories, 7 g protein, 28 g carbohydrates, 25 g total fat, 4 g saturated fat, 4 mg cholesterol, 6 g dietary fiber, 205 mg sodium

tropical fruit salad
with peanut-rum dressing (photo on page 42)

The dried cranberries add a vibrant color accent in this lush and sophisticated fruit salad—a far cry from the canned stuff we had as kids. The dressing is also delicious without the rum, so omit it, if you prefer.

2 TABLESPOONS PEANUT BUTTER

2 TABLESPOONS FRESH ORANGE JUICE

1 TABLESPOON FRESH LIME JUICE

1 TABLESPOON RUM

1/2 TEASPOON LIGHT BROWN SUGAR (OPTIONAL)

2 CUPS FRESH PINEAPPLE CHUNKS

1 NAVEL ORANGE, PEELED AND CUT INTO 1-INCH CHUNKS

1 MANGO, PEELED, HALVED, AND CUT INTO 1-INCH CHUNKS

1 APPLE OR RIPE PEAR, CORED AND CUT INTO 1-INCH CHUNKS

2 BANANAS, SLICED

1/4 CUP SWEETENED DRIED CRANBERRIES

1/4 CUP DRY-ROASTED PEANUTS, COARSELY CHOPPED

1 TABLESPOON CHOPPED FRESH MINT

1. In a small bowl, combine the peanut butter, orange juice, lime juice, rum, and sugar (if using), stirring to blend. Set aside.

2. In a large bowl, combine the pineapple, orange, mango, apple, and bananas. Add the reserved sauce, then sprinkle with the cranberries, peanuts, and mint.

SERVES 6

PER SERVING: 283 calories, 6 g protein, 40 g carbohydrates, 12 g total fat, 2 g saturated fat, 0 mg cholesterol, 7 g dietary fiber, 35 mg sodium

note: If you prefer, serve the fruit salad with the dressing on the side.

side dishes

MASHED SWEET POTATO BAKE
56

BRAISED CARROTS WITH SOY-PEANUT GLAZE
57

SPICY PEANUT GREEN BEANS
58

SPINACH WITH PEANUT SAUCE
59

**GRILLED BELL PEPPERS AND ZUCCHINI
WITH PEANUT ROMESCO SAUCE**
60

INDONESIAN EGGPLANT
62

PEANUT MASHED POTATO CAKES
63

CURRIED CHICORY FRITTERS
64

mashed sweet potato bake

Peanut butter and apple juice add their unique flavor notes to this sweet potato casserole enlivened with cinnamon and nutmeg.

3 TABLESPOONS LIGHT BROWN SUGAR

2 TABLESPOONS APPLE JUICE

2 TABLESPOONS PEANUT BUTTER

1 TABLESPOON NONHYDROGENATED MARGARINE

1/2 TEASPOON CINNAMON

1/2 TEASPOON NUTMEG

1/2 TEASPOON VANILLA EXTRACT

3 LARGE SWEET POTATOES, PEELED AND DICED

SALT AND FRESHLY GROUND BLACK PEPPER

1. In a small bowl, combine 1 tablespoon of the sugar with the apple juice, peanut butter, margarine, cinnamon, nutmeg, and vanilla and blend until smooth. Set aside.

2. Cook the sweet potatoes in a large saucepan of boiling water until tender, 15 to 20 minutes. Drain well and return to the saucepan. Add the reserved peanut butter mixture to the potatoes and season with salt and pepper to taste. Mash until smooth and well combined.

3. Preheat the oven to 400°F. Lightly grease a shallow 1$\frac{1}{2}$-quart baking dish. Transfer the sweet potato mixture to the prepared dish and sprinkle with the remaining 2 tablespoons sugar. Bake until hot, about 30 minutes.

SERVES 4

PER SERVING: 233 calories, 5 g protein, 37 g carbohydrates, 8 g total fat, 2 g saturated fat, 0 mg cholesterol, 6 g dietary fiber, 145 mg sodium

braised carrots with soy-peanut glaze

The thick, flavorful glaze turns everyday carrots into a special treat.

3 TABLESPOONS TAMARI OR
OTHER SOY SAUCE

3 TABLESPOONS PEANUT BUTTER

2 TABLESPOONS PURE MAPLE
SYRUP

1/8 TEASPOON CAYENNE

2/3 CUP WATER

5 TO 6 CARROTS, TRIMMED AND
SLICED DIAGONALLY

1 TABLESPOON EXTRA-VIRGIN
OLIVE OIL

1. In a small bowl, whisk together the tamari, peanut butter, maple syrup, cayenne, and water until smooth. Set aside.

2. Steam or cook the carrots in a pot of boiling salted water until slightly softened, about 5 minutes. Drain well and set aside.

3. Heat the oil in a large skillet over medium heat. Add the carrots, tossing to coat with the oil, then stir in the reserved soy-peanut mixture. Reduce the heat to low and stir to coat the carrots with the sauce. Cover and cook until the carrots are soft and well glazed, 8 to 10 minutes. Serve hot.

SERVES 4

PER SERVING: 195 calories, 6 g protein, 20 g carbohydrates, 11 g total fat, 2 g saturated fat, 0 mg cholesterol, 4 g dietary fiber, 769 mg sodium

spicy peanut green beans

If you don't want the heat of the red-pepper flakes, there's no need to pass on this dish—it's plenty flavorful without them. Mirin is a sweet Japanese cooking wine made from rice. It is available in supermarkets, Asian markets, and natural food stores.

1½ POUNDS GREEN BEANS, TRIMMED

2 TABLESPOONS PEANUT BUTTER

2 TABLESPOONS TAMARI OR OTHER SOY SAUCE

1 TABLESPOON TOASTED SESAME OIL

1 TABLESPOON MIRIN OR WATER

½ TEASPOON SUGAR

2 TABLESPOONS PEANUT OIL

1 LARGE CLOVE GARLIC, MINCED

1 TEASPOON MINCED FRESH GINGER

½ TEASPOON RED-PEPPER FLAKES, OR TO TASTE

1. Steam the green beans just until tender, about 5 minutes. Rinse under cold water to stop the cooking process. Drain and set aside.

2. In a small bowl, combine the peanut butter, tamari, sesame oil, mirin, and sugar and set aside.

3. Heat the peanut oil in a wok or large skillet over medium-high heat. Add the reserved beans in batches and stir-fry for 30 seconds, transferring the cooked beans to a platter.

4. When all the beans have been removed, add the garlic, ginger, and red-pepper flakes to the same pan and stir-fry for 10 seconds. Return the beans to the pan and stir-fry for 30 seconds. Add the reserved peanut butter mixture and stir-fry until the beans are hot and coated with the sauce, about 30 seconds.

SERVES 4

PER SERVING: 217 calories, 6 g protein, 16 g carbohydrates, 15 g total fat, 2 g saturated fat, 0 mg cholesterol, 7 g dietary fiber, 489 mg sodium

spinach with peanut sauce

Combining spinach with a creamy sauce is a universally popular way to enjoy these iron-rich greens—from American creamed spinach to Japanese gomai, a cooked spinach salad that is coated with a ground sesame seed sauce and served at room temperature.

1 POUND FRESH SPINACH, WELL WASHED

³/₄ CUP UNSWEETENED COCONUT MILK

3 TABLESPOONS PEANUT BUTTER

1 TABLESPOON PEANUT OIL

1 TEASPOON GRATED FRESH GINGER

¹/₂ TEASPOON GROUND CUMIN

¹/₈ TEASPOON GROUND OR FRESHLY GRATED NUTMEG

SALT AND FRESHLY GROUND BLACK PEPPER

1. Steam the spinach over boiling water until tender, 2 to 3 minutes. Press any liquid from the spinach and chop it well. Set aside.

2. In a small bowl, combine the coconut milk and peanut butter until blended. Set aside.

3. Heat the oil in a large skillet over medium heat. Add the ginger, cumin, and nutmeg and cook until fragrant, about 30 seconds.

4. Stir in the reserved spinach, the peanut butter mixture, and salt and pepper to taste. Simmer, stirring frequently, until hot and creamy, about 5 to 7 minutes. Serve hot.

SERVES 4

PER SERVING: 268 calories, 7 g protein, 18 g carbohydrates, 22 g total fat, 11 g saturated fat, 0 mg cholesterol, 8 g dietary fiber, 216 mg sodium

grilled bell peppers and zucchini with peanut romesco sauce (photo on page 54)

This version of Romesco sauce uses a fraction of the olive oil that's in the traditional Spanish sauce and substitutes peanut butter for the traditional almonds. If you don't have a grill, you can broil or sauté the vegetables, with delicious results.

4 LARGE RED BELL PEPPERS, QUARTERED LENGTHWISE AND SEEDED

2 TABLESPOONS OLIVE OIL, PLUS MORE FOR GRILLING

1 SMALL RED CHILE, SEEDED AND MINCED

2 TABLESPOONS CHOPPED ONION

1 TABLESPOON CHOPPED GARLIC

1 CAN (14.5 OUNCES) DICED TOMATOES, DRAINED

2 TABLESPOONS RED WINE VINEGAR

1/4 CUP PEANUT BUTTER

SALT AND FRESHLY GROUND BLACK PEPPER

3 SMALL ZUCCHINI, TRIMMED AND HALVED LENGTHWISE

1. Chop 1 bell pepper and set aside the other 3 peppers.

2. Heat 1 tablespoon of the oil in a large skillet over medium heat. Add the chopped bell pepper, chile, onion, and garlic, and cook, covered, for 15 minutes. Stir in the tomatoes and vinegar and cook 15 minutes longer.

3. Transfer the mixture to a food processor or blender and add the peanut butter and salt and pepper to taste. Process until smooth and creamy. Set aside.

4. Toss the zucchini and the remaining 3 bell peppers with enough of the remaining olive oil to coat. Season with salt and pepper and grill until softened and lightly browned, turning once, 5 to 7 minutes per side.

5. While the vegetables are cooking, gently heat the reserved sauce. To serve, transfer the peppers and zucchini to a serving platter and spoon the sauce on top, or serve the sauce on the side.

SERVES 4

PER SERVING: 199 calories, 8 g protein, 24 g carbohydrates, 10 g total fat, 1 g saturated fat, 0 mg cholesterol, 6 g dietary fiber, 290 mg sodium

early origins

The origin of peanut butter can be traced to several different regions of the world. In China, creamy peanut sauces have been around for centuries, while records show that in Africa, peanuts have been ground for stews since at least the 15th century. In America, a creamy peanut porridge was served to soldiers during the Civil War. Peanuts were called goobers then—hence the popular anthem at the time, "Eating Goober Peas."

indonesian eggplant

In the classic Indonesian dish called *Petjel Terong*, the eggplant is usually deep-fried. In this healthier version, the eggplant is baked in the oven with a small amount of olive oil.

1 LARGE EGGPLANT, TRIMMED

2 TABLESPOONS OLIVE OIL

SALT AND FRESHLY GROUND BLACK PEPPER

1 CUP UNSWEETENED COCONUT MILK

1/4 CUP PEANUT BUTTER

1 CLOVE GARLIC, MINCED

1 TABLESPOON LIGHT BROWN SUGAR

1 TABLESPOON FRESH LEMON JUICE

1 TABLESPOON TAMARI OR OTHER SOY SAUCE

1/8 TEASPOON CAYENNE, OR TO TASTE

1 TABLESPOON MINCED FRESH PARSLEY

1. Preheat the oven to 425°F. Halve the eggplant lengthwise, then cut each half crosswise into 1/4-inch-thick slices. Arrange the eggplant slices on a lightly oiled baking sheet, brush them with the olive oil, and season with salt and pepper to taste. Bake, turning once, until softened and browned on both sides, about 15 minutes.

2. While the eggplant is baking, make the sauce. In a medium saucepan, combine the coconut milk, peanut butter, garlic, sugar, lemon juice, tamari, and cayenne. Bring to a boil, then reduce the heat to low and simmer, stirring frequently, until the sauce thickens slightly, about 5 minutes.

3. Arrange the eggplant slices on a platter and top with the sauce. Garnish with the parsley.

SERVES 4

PER SERVING: 367 calories, 8 g protein, 20 g carbohydrates, 31 g total fat, 15 g saturated fat, 0 mg cholesterol, 10 g dietary fiber, 283 mg sodium

peanut mashed potato cakes

Peanut butter enhances the light, sweet flavor of these potato pancakes, made with cold leftover mashed potatoes. The outside becomes crisp and brown, while the inside remains soft. In addition to a great dinner side dish, these cakes also make a terrific breakfast or brunch dish.

1³/₄ CUPS COLD MASHED POTATOES

¹/₄ CUP ALL-PURPOSE FLOUR, PLUS MORE FOR DREDGING

2 TABLESPOONS PEANUT BUTTER

2 SCALLIONS, MINCED

1 TABLESPOON MINCED FRESH PARSLEY

SALT AND FRESHLY GROUND BLACK PEPPER

2 TABLESPOONS OLIVE OIL

1. Place the potatoes in a bowl. Add the ¹/₄ cup flour, peanut butter, scallions, parsley, and salt and pepper to taste. Mix well.

2. Scoop out a spoonful of the potato mixture and, using your hands, shape into a small patty. Repeat until all the mixture is used up. You should have 8 to 10 cakes. Dredge them in the extra flour and set aside.

3. Heat the oil in a large nonstick skillet over medium-high heat. Add the potato cakes, in batches, and cook until crisp and golden brown on both sides, about 10 minutes.

SERVES 4

PER SERVING: 250 calories, 5 g protein, 24 g carbohydrates, 16 g total fat, 3 g saturated fat, 1 mg cholesterol, 3 g dietary fiber, 327 mg sodium

curried chicory fritters

Serve these fritters with applesauce or chutney on the side. If you're not a curry fan, omit the curry powder and add 2 tablespoons of chopped peanuts. For a spicy version, add some cayenne or minced jalapeño.

1 HEAD CHICORY (CURLY ENDIVE), WASHED, TRIMMED, AND CHOPPED

1 SMALL YELLOW ONION, GRATED

2 TABLESPOONS PEANUT BUTTER

½ CUP ALL-PURPOSE FLOUR

1 TEASPOON CURRY POWDER

1 TEASPOON SALT

FRESHLY GROUND BLACK PEPPER

PEANUT OIL

1. Preheat the oven to 250°F. Blanch the chicory in a pot of boiling salted water. Drain well and place in a large bowl. Add the onion and peanut butter and mix well.

2. Stir in the flour, curry powder, salt, and pepper to taste and mix until well combined.

3. Heat a thin layer of oil in a large nonstick skillet over medium heat. Scoop a large spoonful of the vegetable mixture and press it with your hands to pack firmly. Repeat until all of the vegetable mixture is used. Cook the fritters in the hot pan, in batches, until they are golden brown on both sides, about 5 minutes. Add more oil to the pan as necessary.

4. Drain the cooked fritters on paper towels and transfer to the oven to keep warm until all the fritters are cooked. Serve hot.

SERVES 4

PER SERVING (2 FRITTERS): 146 calories, 6 g protein, 20 g carbohydrates, 5 g total fat, 1 g saturated fat, 0 mg cholesterol, 6 g dietary fiber, 630 mg sodium

note: If you prefer a finer texture, puree the vegetable mixture in a food processor before cooking. Other dark greens such as kale, chard, escarole, or spinach may be used instead of the chicory.

march into national peanut month

National Peanut Week was established in 1941, but by 1974 the entire month of March was designated National Nutrition Month, an especially appropriate time to acknowledge the nutritional value of peanuts. Peanut butter is a good source of protein, B-complex vitamins, iron, calcium, magnesium, and potassium.

main dishes

sweet potato and peanut stew

This colorful stew combines sweet potatoes and peanuts with dark red kidney beans for a hearty dish that is both nourishing and delicious.

1 TABLESPOON OLIVE OIL

1 LARGE YELLOW ONION, CHOPPED

1 LARGE RED BELL PEPPER, CHOPPED

1 LARGE CLOVE GARLIC, MINCED

1 TEASPOON LIGHT BROWN SUGAR

1 TEASPOON GRATED FRESH GINGER

$1/2$ TEASPOON GROUND CUMIN

$1/4$ TEASPOON CAYENNE

1 LARGE SWEET POTATO, PEELED AND CUT INTO $1/2$-INCH CHUNKS

1 CAN (14.5 OUNCES) DICED TOMATOES, DRAINED

$1^1/2$ CUPS VEGETABLE STOCK

SALT

$1^1/2$ CUPS COOKED OR ONE 15-OUNCE CAN DARK RED KIDNEY BEANS, DRAINED AND RINSED

$1/2$ CUP PEANUT BUTTER

$1/4$ CUP CHOPPED ROASTED PEANUTS

1. Heat the oil in a large pot over medium heat. Add the onion and cook, covered, until softened, about 5 minutes.

2. Add the bell pepper and garlic. Cover and cook until softened, about 5 minutes.

3. Stir in the sugar, ginger, cumin, and cayenne and cook for 30 seconds. Add the sweet potato and stir to coat with the spices.

4. Stir in the tomatoes and stock, and season with salt to taste. Bring to a boil, then reduce the heat to low, add the kidney beans, and simmer until the vegetables are soft, about 30 minutes.

5. In a small bowl, combine the peanut butter and 1 cup of the liquid from the stew, stirring until blended, then stir it into the stew. Taste to adjust seasonings. Serve hot, sprinkled with chopped peanuts.

SERVES 4

PER SERVING: 496 calories, 19 g protein, 49 g carbohydrates, 28 g total fat, 4 g saturated fat, 0 mg cholesterol, 12 g dietary fiber, 520 mg sodium

curried chickpea stew

For a thicker consistency, scoop out a cup or so of the stew and puree it in a blender or food processor, then stir it back into the pot—or use an immersion blender right in the pot. Serve over brown basmati rice.

1 TABLESPOON OLIVE OIL

1 LARGE YELLOW ONION, DICED

1 LARGE CARROT, HALVED LENGTHWISE AND CUT INTO $1/4$-INCH SLICES

1 LARGE ALL-PURPOSE POTATO, PEELED AND CUT INTO $1/2$-INCH DICE

4 OUNCES GREEN BEANS, CUT INTO 1-INCH PIECES

2 CLOVES GARLIC, MINCED

1 FRESH HOT OR MILD CHILE, SEEDED AND MINCED

1 TABLESPOON CURRY POWDER, OR TO TASTE

1 TEASPOON LIGHT BROWN SUGAR

3 CUPS COOKED OR TWO 15-OUNCE CANS CHICKPEAS, DRAINED AND RINSED

2 CUPS VEGETABLE STOCK OR WATER

1 CAN (14.5 OUNCES) DICED TOMATOES, UNDRAINED

SALT AND FRESHLY GROUND BLACK PEPPER

$1/2$ CUP CREAMY PEANUT BUTTER

1 CUP FROZEN PEAS, THAWED

$1/4$ CUP CHOPPED DRY-ROASTED PEANUTS

$1/4$ CUP CHOPPED PINEAPPLE (OPTIONAL)

1. Heat the oil in a large saucepan over medium heat. Add the onion and carrot and cook, covered, until softened, about 5 minutes. Stir in the potato, green beans, garlic, chile, curry powder, and sugar, and cook for 1 minute, stirring to coat the vegetables with the spices. Add the chickpeas, stock, tomatoes, and salt and pepper to taste. Bring to a boil, then reduce the heat to low.

2. Place the peanut butter in a small bowl and add about 1 cup of the cooking liquid, stirring until smooth. Mix into the stew, then cover and simmer until the vegetables are soft, about 30 minutes.

3. About 10 minutes before the end of the cooking time, remove the lid and add the peas. Simmer uncovered. Serve sprinkled with chopped peanuts and pineapple, if using.

SERVES 6

PER SERVING: 465 calories, 19 g protein, 56 g carbohydrates, 21 g total fat, 3 g saturated fat, 0 mg cholesterol, 14 g dietary fiber, 454 mg sodium

west african vegetable stew

Brimming with vegetables, this flavorful stew is especially good served over rice or couscous or with coarse whole grain bread. Like most stews, this tastes even better the second day, so make it ahead if you can. The crops of peanuts (or groundnuts), sweet potatoes (or yams), and okra can be found throughout western African countries, where stews such as this are often called Groundnut Stew.

1 SWEET POTATO, PEELED AND DICED

1 TABLESPOON PEANUT OIL

1 LARGE YELLOW ONION, CHOPPED

1 GREEN BELL PEPPER, CHOPPED

1 MEDIUM EGGPLANT, DICED

1 CUP SLICED OKRA (FRESH OR FROZEN)

1 CLOVE GARLIC, MINCED

1 CAN (14.5 OUNCES) DICED TOMATOES, UNDRAINED

$1/2$ CUP PEANUT BUTTER

$1^1/_2$ CUPS VEGETABLE STOCK

$1/_4$ TEASPOON CAYENNE, OR TO TASTE

$1/_2$ TEASPOON SALT

$1/_8$ TEASPOON FRESHLY GROUND BLACK PEPPER

1. Place the diced sweet potato in a heat-proof bowl with $\frac{1}{2}$ cup of warm water. Cover and cook in the microwave oven for 5 minutes to soften slightly. Set aside.

2. Heat the oil in a large saucepan over medium heat. Add the onion and bell pepper and cook for 5 minutes. Stir in the eggplant, okra, garlic, and reserved sweet potato. Cover and cook 5 minutes longer, then stir in the tomatoes and cook for a few minutes.

3. In a small bowl, combine the peanut butter and stock, stirring until smooth. Stir the peanut butter mixture into the stew and season with cayenne, salt, and pepper. Simmer until the vegetables are tender, about 30 minutes. For a thicker consistency, scoop out about 1 cup of the stew and puree it in a blender or food processor, then return it to the saucepan.

SERVES 4

PER SERVING: 387 calories, 13 g protein, 37 g carbohydrates, 24 g total fat, 3 g saturated fat, 0 mg cholesterol, 11 g dietary fiber, 843 mg sodium

linguine with spicy peanut pesto

Redolent of garlic, lemongrass, and pungent herbs, this Asian-style pesto makes a fabulous fusion dish when combined with linguine. Most of these ingredients, including the slender, hot Thai chile, are available in supermarkets. Thai basil can be found in Asian markets, as can any of the other ingredients that your regular market may not stock.

2 LARGE CLOVES GARLIC

1 THAI BIRD CHILE, HALVED
LENGTHWISE AND SEEDED

1 STALK LEMONGRASS, WHITE
PART ONLY

1 TEASPOON SUGAR

1/2 TEASPOON SALT

1 CUP THAI BASIL LEAVES

1/2 CUP CILANTRO LEAVES

1/2 CUP PARSLEY LEAVES

1/3 CUP PEANUT BUTTER

3 TABLESPOONS PEANUT OIL OR
OTHER LIGHT FLAVORLESS OIL

2 TABLESPOONS FRESH LIME
JUICE

12 OUNCES LINGUINE

1/2 CUP CHOPPED ROASTED
PEANUTS

1. Combine the garlic, chile, lemongrass, sugar, and salt in a food processor and process to a paste. Add the basil, cilantro, and parsley and process until finely ground. Add the peanut butter, oil, and lime juice and blend thoroughly, scraping down the sides of the bowl as needed. Set aside.

2. Cook the linguine in a large pot of salted water just until tender, about 12 minutes. Drain, reserving about 1/2 cup of the water. Toss the pasta with the sauce, adding a little of the hot pasta water, if necessary, to thin the sauce. Garnish with peanuts and serve immediately.

SERVES 4

PER SERVING: 665 calories, 22 g protein, 75 g carbohydrates, 34 g total fat, 5 g saturated fat, 0 mg cholesterol, 7 g dietary fiber, 353 mg sodium

nutritionally speaking

A 1-ounce serving of peanut butter supplies about 14 percent of the daily recommendation of protein and 8 percent of fiber. It also contains 25 percent of vitamin E, 20 percent of niacin, 12 percent of magnesium, and 10 percent of copper, folate, and potassium that are required daily. Since that same serving portion also contains about 170 calories, many nutritionists recommend that peanut butter be consumed regularly as a nutrient-rich meat alternative—which is its originally intended use.

peanut macaroni pie

Loaded with protein and great flavor, this is a fun version of mac and cheese that kids will love. One-half cup of thawed frozen baby green peas mixed in with the macaroni makes a nice addition.

8 OUNCES ELBOW MACARONI

2 TABLESPOONS OLIVE OIL

1 LARGE YELLOW ONION, CHOPPED

2 CUPS MILK OR SOY MILK

4 OUNCES SILKEN TOFU

$\frac{1}{4}$ CUP PEANUT BUTTER

1 TABLESPOON FRESH LEMON JUICE

$\frac{1}{4}$ TEASPOON MUSTARD POWDER

$\frac{1}{4}$ TEASPOON CAYENNE

PINCH OF NUTMEG

SALT

2 TABLESPOONS MINCED FRESH PARSLEY

$\frac{1}{4}$ CUP BREAD CRUMBS

$\frac{1}{4}$ CUP GROUND PEANUTS

PAPRIKA (OPTIONAL)

1. Cook the macaroni in a pot of salted boiling water until al dente, about 8 minutes. Drain and set aside in a lightly oiled baking dish or a 10-inch deep-dish pie plate.

2. Preheat the oven to 375°F. Heat 1 tablespoon of the oil in a medium skillet over medium heat. Add the onion, cover, and cook until tender, about 5 minutes.

3. In a blender or food processor, combine the onion, milk, tofu, peanut butter, lemon juice, mustard, cayenne, nutmeg, and salt to taste. Blend until smooth. Pour the sauce over the reserved macaroni, add the parsley, and mix well.

4. In a small bowl, combine the bread crumbs and peanuts with the remaining 1 tablespoon oil, stirring to coat. Sprinkle the crumbs onto the macaroni mixture, along with a few shakes of paprika, if using. Cover and bake until hot and bubbly, about 25 minutes. Uncover and bake until the top is lightly browned, about 10 minutes longer.

SERVES 4

PER SERVING: 427 calories, 16 g protein, 38 g carbohydrates, 25 g total fat, 5 g saturated fat, 12 mg cholesterol, 4 g dietary fiber, 153 mg sodium

rice noodles with hoisin-peanut sauce

Deliciously rich and satisfying, chewy rice noodles combine with crisp vegetables and a fragrant, creamy sauce of peanuts, hoisin sauce, lime, and cilantro. Use linguine if rice noodles are unavailable.

8 OUNCES FLAT DRIED RICE NOODLES

$1/3$ CUP PEANUT BUTTER

$1/4$ CUP HOISIN SAUCE

1 CLOVE GARLIC, MINCED

1 TABLESPOON TAMARI OR OTHER SOY SAUCE

2 TEASPOONS FRESH LIME JUICE

1 TEASPOON LIGHT BROWN SUGAR

$1/4$ TEASPOON CAYENNE

$3/4$ CUP WATER

1 TABLESPOON PEANUT OIL

1 SMALL RED ONION, THINLY SLICED

1 SMALL RED BELL PEPPER, SEEDED AND THINLY SLICED

2 TABLESPOONS MINCED FRESH CILANTRO

2 TABLESPOONS CHOPPED ROASTED PEANUTS

1. Soak the noodles in water for 15 minutes. Drain and set aside.

2. In a bowl or food processor, combine the peanut butter, hoisin sauce, garlic, tamari, lime juice, sugar, cayenne, and $1/2$ cup of the water. Blend until smooth. Add as much of the remaining $1/4$ cup water as needed for a creamy saucelike consistency. Set aside.

3. Heat the oil in a skillet over medium-high heat. Add the onion and bell pepper and stir-fry until crisp-tender, 2 to 3 minutes. Add the reserved sauce, reduce the heat to low, and simmer until the sauce is hot. Keep warm.

4. In a large pot of boiling water, cook the rice noodles just until tender, about 1 minute.

Drain, rinse, and return to the pot. Add the sauce and toss to combine. Serve garnished with cilantro and peanuts.

SERVES 4

PER SERVING: 459 calories, 8 g protein, 66 g carbohydrates, 19 g total fat, 3 g saturated fat, 0 mg cholesterol, 4 g dietary fiber, 546 mg sodium

variation: Thin strips of chicken, pork, or beef may be stir-fried with the onion and bell pepper.

note: If you are using fresh rice noodles, omit the soaking instructions.

winter vegetable pot pie

This luscious pot pie is comfort food at its finest—thanks, in part, to the tasty goodness of peanut butter, which enriches the creamy sauce.

FILLING:

1 CUP GREEN BEANS, CUT INTO 1-INCH PIECES

1 CARROT, CHOPPED

1 ALL-PURPOSE POTATO, CUT INTO $1/2$-INCH DICE

1 CUP VEGETABLE STOCK

$1/4$ CUP PEANUT BUTTER

$1^1/2$ TABLESPOONS TAMARI OR OTHER SOY SAUCE

1 TABLESPOON CORNSTARCH DISSOLVED IN 2 TABLESPOONS COLD WATER

$1/4$ TEASPOON DRIED THYME

$1/4$ TEASPOON DRIED TARRAGON (OPTIONAL)

SALT AND FRESHLY GROUND BLACK PEPPER

1 TABLESPOON OLIVE OIL

1 YELLOW ONION, CHOPPED

$3/4$ CUP FROZEN CORN KERNELS, THAWED

$3/4$ CUP FROZEN PEAS, THAWED

CRUST:

$1^1/4$ CUPS ALL-PURPOSE FLOUR

$1/4$ TEASPOON SALT

$1/3$ CUP NONHYDROGENATED MARGARINE

2 TABLESPOONS ICE WATER

FOR THE FILLING:

1. Steam the green beans, carrot, and potato over a pot of boiling water until tender, about 10 minutes. Set aside.

2. In a small saucepan, blend the stock, peanut butter, and tamari, and bring to a boil. Reduce the heat to low and whisk in the cornstarch mixture. Simmer, stirring, until thickened, 1 to 2 minutes. Stir in the thyme and tarragon, if using, and season to taste with salt and pepper. Remove from the heat and set aside.

3. Heat the oil in a medium skillet over medium heat. Add the onion, cover, and cook until softened, about 5 minutes. Remove the onion from the skillet and transfer to a 1$\frac{1}{2}$- to 2-quart casserole dish. Stir in the corn, peas, the reserved green bean mixture, and the reserved sauce. Set aside.

FOR THE CRUST:

1. Preheat the oven to 350°F. In a food processor, combine the flour and salt, pulsing to blend. Add the margarine and process until the mixture is crumbly. With the machine running, slowly add the water and process until the mixture forms a ball.

2. Roll out the dough on a lightly floured surface until it is slightly larger than the rim of the casserole dish.

3. Place the crust over the filled casserole, prick holes in the top with a fork, and crimp the edges.

4. Bake until the filling is hot and bubbling and the crust is browned, about 45 minutes.

SERVES 6

PER SERVING: 323 calories, 8 g protein, 39 g carbohydrates, 16 g total fat, 4 g saturated fat, 0 mg cholesterol, 5 g dietary fiber, 564 mg sodium

variation: Add 1 to 2 cups of diced cooked chicken when combining the vegetables and sauce.

buckwheat noodles with baby spinach and ginger-peanut sauce

Baby spinach, widely available in supermarkets, cooks quickly for a nourishing and delicious meal that can be on the table in minutes.

$1/2$ CUP PEANUT BUTTER

1 CLOVE GARLIC, MINCED

2 TEASPOONS GRATED FRESH GINGER

1 TEASPOON LIGHT BROWN SUGAR

3 TABLESPOONS FRESH LEMON JUICE

2 TABLESPOONS TAMARI OR OTHER SOY SAUCE

1 CUP WATER

1 TABLESPOON PEANUT OIL

3 CUPS BABY SPINACH

SALT AND FRESHLY GROUND BLACK PEPPER

12 OUNCES BUCKWHEAT SOBA NOODLES

1. In a food processor, combine the peanut butter, garlic, ginger, and sugar. Add the lemon juice, tamari, and $1/2$ cup of the water. Blend until smooth. Transfer the mixture to a saucepan and stir in the remaining $1/2$ cup water. Heat over low heat, stirring until it is hot. Keep it warm.

2. Heat the oil in a large skillet over medium-high heat, add the spinach, and sauté until wilted, about 1 minute. Season with salt and pepper to taste.

3. Cook the soba noodles according to the package directions. Drain well and transfer to a serving bowl. Add the spinach and the peanut sauce and toss gently to combine. Serve hot.

SERVES 4

PER SERVING: 562 calories, 22 g protein, 75 g carbohydrates, 24 g total fat, 3 g saturated fat, 0 mg cholesterol, 4 g dietary fiber, 1,239 mg sodium

double-peanut burgers

Peanut butter and peanuts give these burgers a double-peanut punch. Instead of cooking the burgers on top of the stove, they may be baked in the oven. To do so, arrange them on a lightly oiled baking sheet and bake at 350°F, turning once, until browned on both sides, about 25 to 30 minutes. Serve topped with a brown sauce, ketchup, chutney, or salsa. Or—and this gets my vote—try them with the Ginger-Peanut Sauce (see the opposite page) for even more peanut flavor.

1 SMALL YELLOW ONION, COARSELY CHOPPED

2 CLOVES GARLIC

1 CUP COOKED LENTILS, WELL DRAINED

$1/2$ CUP GROUND PEANUTS

$1/2$ CUP CHOPPED WALNUTS OR PECANS

$1/2$ CUP DRIED BREAD CRUMBS

3 TABLESPOONS PEANUT BUTTER

2 TABLESPOONS TAMARI OR OTHER SOY SAUCE

1 TABLESPOON MINCED FRESH PARSLEY

$1/4$ TEASPOON CAYENNE (OPTIONAL)

3 TABLESPOONS OLIVE OIL

1. Preheat the oven to 350°F. In a food processor, combine the onion, garlic, lentils, peanuts, and walnuts, pulsing to blend while leaving some texture. Add the bread crumbs, peanut butter, tamari, parsley, and cayenne, if using. Pulse until the mixture is well combined. Shape the mixture into 4 patties and place on a platter. Refrigerate for 30 minutes.

2. Heat the oil in a skillet over medium heat, add the patties, and cook until browned on both sides, turning once, about 4 minutes per side.

SERVES 4

PER SERVING: 463 calories, 16 g protein, 30 g carbohydrates, 33 g total fat, 4 g saturated fat, 0 mg cholesterol, 8 g dietary fiber, 597 mg sodium

harvest medley stuffed squash (photo on page 66)

Use a dense, sweet, orange-fleshed squash such as buttercup, acorn, or kabocha for the best results. This flavorful and colorful dish makes an attractive entrée for a Thanksgiving dinner.

1 TABLESPOON OLIVE OIL

1 YELLOW ONION, MINCED

2 CLOVES GARLIC, MINCED

2 CUPS COOKED WHITE OR BROWN RICE

1 CUP COOKED WILD RICE

1/3 CUP PEANUT BUTTER

1/4 CUP SWEETENED DRIED CRANBERRIES

3 TABLESPOONS CHOPPED DRY-ROASTED PEANUTS

1 TABLESPOON MINCED FRESH PARSLEY

1 TEASPOON DRIED TARRAGON

SALT AND FRESHLY GROUND BLACK PEPPER

1 LARGE WINTER SQUASH, HALVED AND SEEDED (SUCH AS BUTTERCUP, ACORN, OR KABOCHA)

1 1/2 CUPS HOT WATER

1. Preheat the oven to 350°F. Heat the oil in a large skillet over medium heat. Add the onion, cover, and cook until softened, about 5 minutes. Add the garlic and cook until fragrant, about 30 seconds. Stir in the rice, wild rice, peanut butter, cranberries, peanuts, parsley, tarragon, and salt and pepper to taste. Mix well and spoon the mixture into the squash cavities.

2. Place the squash halves in a baking dish stuffing sides up. Add the water to the bottom of the baking dish and cover tightly with a lid or aluminum foil. Bake until the squash is tender, about 1 1/2 hours.

SERVES 4

PER SERVING: 487 calories, 14 g protein, 69 g carbohydrates, 21 g total fat, 3 g saturated fat, 0 mg cholesterol, 8 g dietary fiber, 65 mg sodium

peanut facts and trivia

- One acre of peanuts can produce enough peanut butter for 30,000 sandwiches.

- Peanuts are not really nuts—they are legumes, like beans and peas.

- Each American eats nearly 4 pounds of peanut butter per year, for a nationwide total of about 8 million pounds.

- Two United States presidents were peanut farmers: Thomas Jefferson and Jimmy Carter.

- Peanut butter is naturally cholesterol free and low in saturated fat.

- According to the National Peanut Board, approximately 540 peanuts are used to make one 12-ounce jar of peanut butter.

- Peanut butter is the primary use of America's peanut crop.

- It is estimated that nearly 90 percent of US households have a jar of peanut butter in their kitchens.

sweet and spicy stuffed peppers

Salsa and peanut butter join forces in these colorful stuffed peppers that are a little spicy, a little sweet, and 100 percent delicious.

6 RED BELL PEPPERS

1 TABLESPOON OLIVE OIL

1 SMALL YELLOW ONION, CHOPPED

2 CUPS COOKED WHITE OR BROWN RICE

1½ CUPS COOKED OR ONE 15.5-OUNCE CAN DARK RED KIDNEY BEANS, DRAINED AND RINSED

1 CUP TOMATO SALSA

¼ CUP PEANUT BUTTER

2 TABLESPOONS MINCED CANNED JALAPEÑOS

1 TABLESPOON MINCED FRESH PARSLEY

1 TEASPOON LIGHT BROWN SUGAR

SALT AND FRESHLY GROUND BLACK PEPPER

½ CUP APPLE JUICE OR WATER

1. Preheat the oven to 350°F. Slice off the tops of the peppers, reserve and set aside. Remove the seeds and membranes of the peppers. Plunge the peppers into a pot of boiling water and cook until slightly softened, about 3 minutes. Remove from the water and drain, cut side down. Chop the pepper tops and set aside.

2. Heat the oil in a large skillet over medium heat. Add the onion and reserved chopped pepper tops and cook until softened, about 5 minutes.

3. In a large bowl, combine the onion mixture with the rice, beans, salsa, peanut butter, jalapeños, parsley, sugar, and salt and pepper to taste. Mix well.

4. Fill the pepper cavities evenly with the rice mixture, packing tightly. Place upright in a baking dish. Add the apple juice to the baking dish, cover tightly, and bake until the peppers are tender and the stuffing is hot, about 40 minutes.

SERVES 6

PER SERVING: 283 calories, 10 g protein, 42 g carbohydrates, 9 g total fat, 1 g saturated fat, 0 mg cholesterol, 7 g dietary fiber, 239 mg sodium

variation: Ground beef or turkey may be used to replace the kidney beans, if desired.

szechuan stir-fry with fiery peanut sauce

Vary the vegetables according to your personal taste and their availability. The amount of heat in this dish can be controlled by the amount of red-pepper flakes added. Strips of extra-firm tofu are a pleasant foil for the spicy sauce.

$1/2$ CUP WATER

$1/4$ CUP PEANUT BUTTER

$1/4$ CUP TAMARI OR OTHER SOY SAUCE

2 TABLESPOONS RICE VINEGAR

2 TEASPOONS LIGHT BROWN SUGAR

1 TEASPOON KETCHUP

1 CLOVE GARLIC, MINCED

1 TEASPOON GRATED FRESH GINGER

1 TEASPOON RED-PEPPER FLAKES, OR TO TASTE

1 TEASPOON CORNSTARCH DISSOLVED IN 1 TABLESPOON WATER

2 TABLESPOONS PEANUT OIL

8 OUNCES EXTRA-FIRM TOFU, DRAINED, PRESSED, AND CUT INTO $1/2$-INCH STRIPS

1 LARGE YELLOW ONION, HALVED LENGTHWISE AND THINLY SLICED

2 CUPS BROCCOLI FLORETS, BLANCHED

1 RED BELL PEPPER, CUT INTO THIN STRIPS

2 CUPS THINLY SLICED NAPA CABBAGE

1 CUP THINLY SLICED FRESH SHIITAKE MUSHROOMS

6 CUPS COOKED RICE

$1/4$ CUP ROASTED PEANUTS, CHOPPED (OPTIONAL)

1. In a bowl, a food processor, or a blender, combine the water, peanut butter, tamari, vinegar, sugar, ketchup, garlic, ginger, and red-pepper flakes, and blend well.

2. Pour the mixture into a saucepan and bring to a boil. Reduce the heat to low and simmer for 5 minutes, stirring occasionally. Add the cornstarch mixture and cook, stirring, until the sauce thickens. Remove from the heat and set aside.

3. Heat the oil in a large skillet or wok over medium-high heat. Add the tofu and stir-fry until golden brown, about 3 minutes. Remove with a slotted spoon and set aside. Add the onion, broccoli, and bell pepper, and stir-fry for 3 minutes. Add the cabbage and mushrooms and stir-fry 3 minutes longer, or until the vegetables soften. Return the tofu to the skillet. Add the sauce and stir-fry to coat the vegetables. Serve over the rice and top with the chopped peanuts, if using.

SERVES 6

PER SERVING: 200 calories, 11 g protein, 12 g carbohydrates, 14 g total fat, 2 g saturated fat, 0 mg cholesterol, 4 g dietary fiber, 661 mg sodium

variation: One of the great things about stir-fries is that you can add just about anything you want. Instead of the tofu, add shrimp or strips of chicken, beef, or pork if you like.

sandwiches

pb&j revisited

The lunch box favorite gets a healthy makeover with whole grain bread, fruit-sweetened jam, and natural organic peanut butter.

4 SLICES WHOLE GRAIN OR
SPROUTED BREAD

$\frac{1}{4}$ CUP NATURAL ORGANIC
PEANUT BUTTER

$\frac{1}{4}$ CUP FRUIT-SWEETENED
STRAWBERRY JAM

1. Spread 2 slices of the bread with the peanut butter.

2. Spread the remaining 2 slices of bread with the jam and place them on top of the peanut butter slices, filling sides in. Slice diagonally.

SERVES 2

PER SERVING: 408 calories, 14 g protein, 45 g carbohydrates, 22 g total fat, 3 g saturated fat, 0 mg cholesterol, 8 g dietary fiber, 333 mg sodium

kid's corner: peanut butter party

Here's a way to keep your kids and their friends occupied and provide a healthy snack at the same time: Have a peanut butter sandwich-making contest. Put all the ingredients on a table: bread, peanut butter, jelly, sliced fruit, raisins, potato chips, and anything else you want to include. Award prizes for the most creative, most nutritious, most unusual, etc.—and let the kids do the voting. Then let them eat what they made.

IMPORTANT: Check with parents to make sure none of the children invited to the gathering is allergic to peanuts.

grilled peanut butter and banana sandwich

Celebrate Elvis's birthday on January 8 with his favorite sandwich, and eat it the way he reportedly did: with a knife and fork.

2 SMALL RIPE BANANAS

2 TABLESPOONS NONHYDROGENATED MARGARINE

4 SLICES WHITE BREAD

$\frac{1}{4}$ CUP PEANUT BUTTER

1. Place the bananas in a bowl and mash them with a fork. Set aside.

2. Spread the margarine on each slice of bread and place them, margarine side down, on a flat work surface. Spread the peanut butter on 2 slices of the bread and the mashed banana on top of the peanut butter. Top with the remaining 2 bread slices, margarine side up.

3. Place the sandwiches on a griddle or large nonstick skillet and fry, turning once, until golden brown on both sides, about 4 minutes. Cut diagonally.

SERVES 2

PER SERVING: 544 calories, 13 g protein, 55 g carbohydrates, 32 g total fat, 7 g saturated fat, 0 mg cholesterol, 7 g dietary fiber, 538 mg sodium

flower power peanut butter sandwich

Sunflower seeds add crunch to this nutritional peanut butter powerhouse made with whole grain bread, raisins, and carrots. The optional maple syrup adds just a hint of sweetness.

1/2 CUP PEANUT BUTTER

1/4 CUP FINELY SHREDDED CARROT

2 TABLESPOONS SUNFLOWER SEEDS

2 TABLESPOONS RAISINS

2 TEASPOONS PURE MAPLE SYRUP (OPTIONAL)

4 SLICES WHOLE GRAIN OR SPROUTED BREAD

1. In a small bowl, combine the peanut butter, carrot, sunflower seeds, raisins, and maple syrup, if using. Blend well.

2. Spread the peanut butter mixture on 2 slices of the bread. Top each with the remaining 2 bread slices. Cut diagonally.

SERVES 2

PER SERVING: 676 calories, 25 g protein, 51 g carbohydrates, 46 g total fat, 6 g saturated fat, 0 mg cholesterol, 11 g dietary fiber, 415 mg sodium

open-face peanut butter and tomato broil

Hot and tasty, this open-face sandwich is a sophisticated way to enjoy peanut butter. For a "PB&T" sandwich with more zing, top the peanut butter with spicy-hot tomato salsa instead of the tomato slices.

2 ENGLISH MUFFINS, SPLIT

¼ CUP PEANUT BUTTER

4 SLICES LARGE RIPE TOMATO

SALT AND FRESHLY GROUND
BLACK PEPPER

1. Preheat the broiler. Spread the cut sides of the muffins with the peanut butter and place cut side up on a baking sheet.

2. Top each muffin half with a tomato slice and season with salt and pepper to taste. Place under the broiler until hot and lightly browned, about 2 minutes. Serve at once.

SERVES 2

PER SERVING: 372 calories, 14 g protein, 36 g carbohydrates, 21 g total fat, 3 g saturated fat, 0 mg cholesterol, 5 g dietary fiber, 342 mg sodium

giant sandwich

The world's largest peanut butter and jelly sandwich weighed close to 900 pounds. It contained 144 pounds of jelly, 350 pounds of peanut butter, and 400 pounds of bread. It was created in Oklahoma City, Oklahoma, on September 7, 2002, at the governor's mansion for the governor's annual Septemberfest event. The sandwich was made by the Oklahoma Peanut Commission and the Oklahoma Wheat Commission to spotlight peanuts and wheat—Oklahoma's top crops.

peanut butter waldorf wraps

The classic Waldorf salad gets a new look—made with peanut butter and wrapped inside a soft tortilla. I like a sweeter apple in this recipe, such as Fuji, Delicious, or Gala.

2 APPLES, PEELED AND CORED

1 TABLESPOON FRESH LEMON JUICE

1/3 CUP GOLDEN RAISINS

1/2 CUP FINELY MINCED CELERY

2 SCALLIONS, FINELY MINCED

1/2 CUP CHOPPED WALNUTS OR PEANUTS

1/3 CUP SMOOTH OR CRUNCHY PEANUT BUTTER

1/4 CUP REGULAR OR SOY MAYONNAISE

1 TEASPOON SUGAR (OPTIONAL)

SALT AND FRESHLY GROUND BLACK PEPPER

4 FLOUR TORTILLAS

1 CUP SHREDDED ICEBERG LETTUCE

1. Shred the apples or cut them into very thin slices and place them in a large bowl. Add the lemon juice and toss to coat. Drain the liquid from the apples, then add the raisins, celery, scallions, and nuts.

2. In a small bowl, combine the peanut butter, mayonnaise, and sugar, if using, until blended. Spoon just enough of the dressing into the apple mixture to bind the ingredients together, stirring to mix well. Season to taste with salt and pepper. Reserve the remaining dressing to spread on the tortillas.

3. Place the tortillas on a flat work surface and spread the remaining dressing on them. Divide the apple mixture across the lower third of each tortilla, along with the shredded lettuce.

4. Roll up the sandwiches and use a serrated knife to cut them in half.

SERVES 4

PER SERVING: 677 calories, 15 g protein, 56 g carbohydrates, 47 g total fat, 6 g saturated fat, 7 mg cholesterol, 8 g dietary fiber, 397 mg sodium

variation: Chopped or shredded cooked turkey may be added to the apple mixture.

roasted eggplant pita with garlicky lemon-peanut sauce

This yummy sandwich filling is inspired by baba ghanoush, a Middle Eastern eggplant spread made with sesame butter (also called tahini). If you prefer an eggplant spread over sliced eggplant, cut the eggplant in half lengthwise and roast, cut side down, on a lightly oiled baking sheet until soft, then scoop out the middle and add it to the peanut butter mixture.

1 MEDIUM EGGPLANT, TRIMMED

1 TABLESPOON OLIVE OIL

SALT AND FRESHLY GROUND
BLACK PEPPER

3 TABLESPOONS PEANUT BUTTER

1 TABLESPOON FRESH LEMON
JUICE

1 TABLESPOON TAMARI OR OTHER
SOY SAUCE

1 CLOVE GARLIC, MINCED

$1/4$ TEASPOON CAYENNE, OR TO
TASTE

2 LARGE PITA LOAVES, HALVED

1. Preheat the oven to 425°F. Quarter the eggplant lengthwise, then cut each quarter crosswise into $1/4$-inch-thick slices. Arrange the eggplant slices on a lightly oiled baking sheet and brush with the olive oil. Sprinkle with salt and pepper to taste and bake, turning once, until softened and browned on both sides, about 15 minutes.

2. In a bowl or food processor, combine the peanut butter, lemon juice, tamari, garlic, and cayenne. Blend until smooth.

3. Allow the eggplant to cool, then mix into the sauce. Stuff the pitas with the eggplant mixture and serve at once.

SERVES 2

PER SERVING: 466 calories, 16 g protein, 55 g carbohydrates, 24 g total fat, 3 g saturated fat, 0 mg cholesterol, 15 g dietary fiber, 862 mg sodium

thai vegetable wraps (photo on page 90)

These wraps envelop crisp fresh vegetables and a zesty sauce for a yummy lunch or a light supper.

1/4 CUP PEANUT BUTTER

2 TABLESPOONS UNSWEETENED COCONUT MILK

2 TEASPOONS TAMARI OR OTHER SOY SAUCE

2 TEASPOONS FRESH LIME JUICE

2 TEASPOONS LIGHT BROWN SUGAR

1 TEASPOON CHILE PASTE, OR TO TASTE

1 CUP SHREDDED LETTUCE

1/2 CUP SHREDDED CARROT

1/4 CUP CHOPPED RED BELL PEPPER

1/4 CUP BEAN SPROUTS

2 TABLESPOONS FINELY MINCED RED ONION

2 PIECES LAVASH FLATBREAD OR FLOUR TORTILLAS

1. In a small bowl, combine the peanut butter, coconut milk, tamari, lime juice, sugar, and chile paste. Blend well.

2. In a medium bowl, combine the lettuce, carrot, bell pepper, bean sprouts, and onion. Toss to combine.

3. Spread the peanut mixture onto each flatbread, dividing evenly. Top with the vegetable mixture, spreading it on the lower third of each wrap.

4. Roll up the sandwiches and use a serrated knife to cut them in half. Serve at once.

SERVES 2

PER SERVING: 329 calories, 12 g protein, 23 g carbohydrates, 24 g total fat, 6 g saturated fat, 0 mg cholesterol, 7 g dietary fiber, 537 mg sodium

variation: As an additional filling, cooked shrimp or thinly sliced or shredded roast beef, chicken, or pork may be added.

a lot of sandwiches

Before the age of 18, the average American child consumes 1,500

peanut butter and jelly sandwiches.

breakfast and beyond

apple–peanut butter pancakes

Apple slices spread with peanut butter is a favorite healthy snack. This popular flavor combo is just as fabulous in these great-tasting pancakes.

1½ CUPS ALL-PURPOSE FLOUR

1 TABLESPOON SUGAR

2 TEASPOONS BAKING POWDER

¼ TEASPOON SALT

1½ CUPS MILK OR SOY MILK

½ CUP APPLE JUICE

3 TABLESPOONS PEANUT BUTTER

1 TEASPOON VANILLA EXTRACT

1 LARGE APPLE, PEELED, CORED, AND CHOPPED

2 TABLESPOONS CHOPPED DRY-ROASTED PEANUTS

1. In a large bowl, combine the flour, sugar, baking powder, and salt.

2. In a blender, combine the milk, apple juice, peanut butter, and vanilla and blend until smooth. Pour into the flour mixture, stirring with a few swift strokes until just moist. Fold in the chopped apple and peanuts.

3. Preheat the oven to 200°F. Lightly oil a griddle or non-stick skillet and heat until hot. For each pancake, ladle about ¼ cup of the batter onto the griddle or skillet. Cook on one side until small bubbles appear on the top of the pancakes, about 2 minutes. Flip the pancakes with a spatula and cook until the second side is lightly browned, about 1 minute longer. Repeat with the remaining batter. Keep the cooked pancakes warm in the oven while preparing the remaining pancakes.

SERVES 4

PER SERVING (2 PANCAKES): 380 calories, 13 g protein, 55 g carbohydrates, 13 g total fat, 3 g saturated fat, 9 mg cholesterol, 3 g dietary fiber, 414 mg sodium

ginger-peanut scones

These tender scones taste best on the day they are made. For a more pronounced ginger-peanut flavor, add some finely minced crystallized ginger and chopped roasted peanuts to the dough.

2 CUPS UNBLEACHED ALL-PURPOSE FLOUR

1/2 CUP SUGAR

2 TEASPOONS CREAM OF TARTAR

1 TEASPOON BAKING SODA

3/4 TEASPOON SALT

1 TEASPOON GROUND GINGER

1/2 CUP PEANUT BUTTER

1/4 CUP NONHYDROGENATED MARGARINE

1/4 CUP PLUS 2 TEASPOONS MILK OR SOY MILK

1 EGG OR BLENDED EGG SUBSTITUTE FOR 1 EGG (SEE NOTE, PAGE 109)

1. Preheat the oven to 400°F. Lightly grease and flour a baking sheet.

2. In a bowl, sift together the flour, sugar, cream of tartar, baking soda, salt, and ginger. Using a pastry blender, cut in the peanut butter and margarine until the mixture resembles coarse crumbs.

3. In a separate bowl, combine the milk and egg and mix until smooth. Stir into the flour mixture until just blended. Do not overwork.

4. Divide the dough in half and transfer to a floured surface. Using a rolling pin, flatten each piece of dough to 1/2-inch thickness. Cut the dough into 3-inch triangles and place on the prepared baking sheet. Bake for 12 minutes, or until golden brown. Cool slightly. Serve warm.

MAKES 12

PER SCONE: 220 calories, 6 g protein, 26 g carbohydrates, 11 g total fat, 3 g saturated fat, 18 mg cholesterol, 1 g dietary fiber, 325 mg sodium

maple-peanut butter waffles (photo on page 102)

Treat yourself to these yummy waffles, and top with the Peanut Buttery Maple Syrup (see the opposite page) to amplify the flavors.

1/2 CUP PEANUT BUTTER

2 TABLESPOONS NONHYDROGENATED MARGARINE

1¼ CUPS MILK OR SOY MILK

¼ CUP PURE MAPLE SYRUP

1 TEASPOON VANILLA EXTRACT

1½ CUPS ALL-PURPOSE FLOUR

3 TEASPOONS BAKING POWDER

¼ TEASPOON SALT

1. In a large bowl, cream together the peanut butter and margarine. Add the milk, maple syrup, and vanilla and blend until smooth.

2. In a separate bowl, sift together the flour, baking powder, and salt. Add to the peanut butter mixture and stir until smooth.

3. Preheat the oven to 200°F. Preheat a waffle maker. Pour about ³/₄ cup of the batter onto the waffle maker, spreading toward the edges if necessary, and cook according to the manufacturer's instructions. Repeat until the remaining batter is used up. Keep the cooked waffles warm in the oven while preparing the rest.

SERVES 4 (8 SMALL OR 4 LARGE WAFFLES)

PER SERVING: 542 calories, 16 g protein, 59 g carbohydrates, 28 g total fat, 6 g saturated fat, 8 mg cholesterol, 4 g dietary fiber, 615 mg sodium

peanut buttery maple syrup

This richly decadent syrup, perfect with the waffles, is also great on ice cream.

½ CUP PURE MAPLE SYRUP

¼ CUP PEANUT BUTTER

1 TABLESPOON
NONHYDROGENATED MARGARINE

In a small saucepan over low heat, combine the maple syrup, peanut butter, and margarine, stirring frequently until warm and well blended.

SERVES 8 (1 SCANT CUP)

PER SERVING: 141 calories, 3 g protein, 16 g carbohydrates, 8 g total fat, 1 g saturated fat, 0 mg cholesterol, 1 g dietary fiber, 42 mg sodium

cranberry-peanut butter muffins

Bejeweled with sweet-tart cranberries, the only thing better than savoring the aroma of these fresh-baked fragrant muffins is biting into one. Loaded with protein and calcium, they are a good choice for breakfast or a between-meal snack served with coffee or tea. For a less sweet muffin, use ⅓ cup of brown sugar.

⅓ CUP PEANUT BUTTER

3 TABLESPOONS PEANUT OIL

1 CUP MILK OR SOY MILK

1 EGG OR BLENDED EGG
SUBSTITUTE FOR 1 EGG (SEE NOTE)

½ CUP LIGHT BROWN SUGAR, OR
LESS

1¾ CUPS ALL-PURPOSE FLOUR

2½ TEASPOONS BAKING POWDER

½ TEASPOON SALT

¾ TEASPOON GROUND CINNAMON

¼ TEASPOON GROUND ALLSPICE

½ CUP SWEETENED DRIED
CRANBERRIES

1. Preheat the oven to 400°F. Lightly grease a muffin pan.

2. Blend the peanut butter and oil in a large bowl. Add the milk, egg, and sugar and blend until smooth.

3. In a separate bowl, combine the flour, baking powder, salt, cinnamon, and allspice. Stir into the peanut butter mixture until just blended. Fold in the cranberries, then transfer the batter into the prepared muffin pan, filling the cups about two-thirds full.

4. Bake until golden brown and a toothpick inserted into a muffin comes out clean, 15 to 18 minutes. Cool in the pan for 5 to 10 minutes. Serve warm.

MAKES 12

PER MUFFIN: 181 calories, 5 g protein, 21 g carbohydrates, 9 g total fat, 2 g saturated fat, 20 mg cholesterol, 2 g dietary fiber, 216 mg sodium

note: For those who wish to avoid eggs in baking, a number of choices are available. One option is a product found at natural food stores called Ener-G Egg Replacer, made from vegetable starch. To replace 1 egg, blend 1¼ teaspoons of the powder with 2 tablespoons of water. Another option is ground flaxseeds. To replace 1 egg, combine 1 tablespoon of ground flaxseeds with 3 tablespoons of water in a blender and blend until the mixture thickens, about 1 minute.

peanutty granola with dried cranberries

Bursting with seeds, nuts, and whole grain oats, this granola is a protein powerhouse. The cranberries add dazzling color and a sweet-tart accent, as well as potassium. This granola is too delicious to be limited to breakfast. Sprinkle it on fruit salads, yogurt, ice cream, and more.

2 CUPS OLD-FASHIONED ROLLED OATS

1/4 CUP SUNFLOWER SEEDS

1/4 CUP GROUND FLAXSEEDS

1/2 CUP PEANUT BUTTER

1/2 CUP PURE MAPLE SYRUP

1 TABLESPOON PEANUT OIL

1/2 CUP COARSELY CHOPPED UNSALTED PEANUTS

1/2 CUP SWEETENED DRIED CRANBERRIES

1. Preheat the oven to 250°F. Lightly oil a 10 × 15-inch baking pan and set aside. In a large bowl, combine the oats, sunflower seeds, and flaxseeds.

2. In a blender or small bowl, combine the peanut butter, maple syrup, and oil until well blended. Pour over the oats mixture and stir well until coated.

3. Spread the mixture into the prepared pan and bake, stirring every 15 to 20 minutes, until the granola is dry and crumbly, about 2 hours. Remove from the oven and set aside to cool.

4. Once the mixture is cool, stir in the peanuts and cranberries. This granola can be stored in an airtight container for 2 weeks in the refrigerator.

MAKES 4 CUPS

PER SERVING (1/3 CUP): 263 calories, 8 g protein, 30 g carbohydrates, 14 g total fat, 2 g saturated fat, 0 mg cholesterol, 5 g dietary fiber, 28 mg sodium

"Man cannot live by bread alone.

He must have peanut butter."

—Bill Cosby

peanut butter banana bread

One taste will tell you this isn't your everyday banana bread. This one has the added goodness of creamy peanut butter and chopped roasted peanuts.

1 CUP MILK OR SOY MILK

1 CUP SUGAR

¾ CUP PEANUT BUTTER   *½* *— light kraft kind.*

1 TEASPOON VANILLA EXTRACT

2 LARGE RIPE BANANAS, CHOPPED   *3*

2¼ CUPS ALL-PURPOSE FLOUR   *ww*

2 TEASPOONS BAKING POWDER

1 TEASPOON CINNAMON

~~¼ TEASPOON SALT~~   *thin sliced almonds*

½ CUP CHOPPED ROASTED PEANUTS   *no→*   *2 Tbsp egg whites*

1. Preheat the oven to 350°F. Lightly oil a 9 × 5-inch loaf pan and set it aside.

2. In a blender or food processor, combine the milk, sugar, peanut butter, vanilla, and 1 banana and blend until smooth.

3. In a large bowl, sift together the flour, baking powder, cinnamon, and salt. Add the banana mixture and mix well. Fold in the peanuts and the remaining banana.

4. Fill the prepared pan with the batter and bake until a toothpick inserted into the center comes out clean, about 45 minutes. Cool in the pan before slicing.

MAKES 1 LOAF (16 SERVINGS)

PER SERVING: 250 calories, 7 g protein, 35 g carbohydrates, 10 g total fat, 2 g saturated fat, 2 mg cholesterol, 3 g dietary fiber, 121 mg sodium

19 July/07 - rainy + cool
- tasty, bit dense
- good c̄ jam

4 Nov/15
for Sadee!
used ½ c. banana ½ c. applesauce
1 egg, ½ c. br. sugar 3/4 c. pb, no cin
or salt
or vanilla
→ super delicious light texture

oatmeal with a swirl of peanut butter

When is oatmeal more than just oatmeal? When it is enhanced by the creamy taste of peanut butter for a nutrient-rich, stick-to-your-ribs breakfast.

4 CUPS WATER

2 CUPS OLD-FASHIONED ROLLED OATS

3/4 TEASPOON GROUND CINNAMON

PINCH OF SALT

1/4 CUP PEANUT BUTTER

2 TABLESPOONS PURE MAPLE SYRUP

1 TABLESPOON NONHYDROGENATED MARGARINE

1. Bring the water to a boil in a medium saucepan over high heat. Reduce the heat to low and stir in the oats, cinnamon, and salt. Simmer for 5 minutes, stirring occasionally.

2. Remove the saucepan from the heat, cover, and let stand for 2 to 3 minutes.

3. In a small saucepan, combine the peanut butter, maple syrup, and margarine over medium-low heat, stirring to blend.

4. To serve, spoon the oatmeal into 4 bowls and garnish each with a swirl of the peanut butter mixture.

SERVES 4

PER SERVING: 358 calories, 11 g protein, 45 g carbohydrates, 16 g total fat, 3 g saturated fat, 0 mg cholesterol, 7 g dietary fiber, 74 mg sodium

taste of the tropics smoothie

Smoothies are a great way to use bananas that are beginning to get too ripe. Just peel them, cut into chunks, and store in the freezer. That way, you can have cold, rich smoothies at a moment's notice.

1 LARGE FROZEN RIPE BANANA, CUT INTO CHUNKS

$1/2$ CUP FRESH OR CANNED PINEAPPLE CHUNKS

$3/4$ CUP PINEAPPLE JUICE

2 TABLESPOONS PEANUT BUTTER

1 TABLESPOON MAPLE SYRUP (OPTIONAL)

1 TEASPOON VANILLA EXTRACT

4 TO 6 ICE CUBES

In a blender, combine the banana, pineapple chunks, pineapple juice, peanut butter, maple syrup (if using), vanilla, and ice cubes. Blend until smooth. Serve immediately.

SERVES 2

PER SERVING: 281 calories, 6 g protein, 45 g carbohydrates, 10 g total fat, 1 g saturated fat, 0 mg cholesterol, 5 g dietary fiber, 39 mg sodium

handcrafted granola bars

Homemade granola bars are so quick and easy, you'll wonder why you never made them before. You can customize them to include favorite ingredients, such as peanut butter and omega-3-rich flaxseeds. Be sure to use ground flaxseeds, available at natural food stores, for this recipe. If you buy whole flaxseeds, grind them at home in a spice grinder.

2½ CUPS OLD-FASHIONED ROLLED OATS

1 CUP SUNFLOWER SEEDS

¾ CUP GROUND FLAXSEEDS

½ CUP CHOPPED UNSALTED PEANUTS

½ CUP RAISINS

½ CUP FLAKED COCONUT

½ CUP PURE MAPLE SYRUP

⅔ CUP PEANUT BUTTER

⅓ CUP NONHYDROGENATED MARGARINE

⅓ CUP LIGHT BROWN SUGAR

1 TABLESPOON APPLE JUICE

2 TEASPOONS VANILLA EXTRACT

1 TEASPOON BAKING SODA

1. Preheat the oven to 325°F. Lightly grease a 9-inch square baking pan.

2. In a large mixing bowl, combine the oats, sunflower seeds, flaxseeds, peanuts, raisins, and coconut. Set aside.

3. In a saucepan, combine the maple syrup, peanut butter, margarine, and sugar. Cook over medium heat, stirring constantly, until the sugar is dissolved and the mixture is smooth. Stir in the apple juice, vanilla, and baking soda and remove from the heat.

4. Pour the peanut butter mixture into the oats mixture and stir until well combined. Transfer the mixture to the prepared pan. Place a piece of plastic wrap on top and use your hands to press the mixture very firmly and evenly into the pan. Remove the plastic wrap and bake for 20 minutes. Cool to room temperature, then cover and refrigerate until firm. Use a sharp knife to cut into bars and store them in the refrigerator for up to 2 weeks.

MAKES 18

PER BAR: 309 calories, 9 g protein, 27 g carbohydrates, 20 g total fat, 4 g saturated fat, 0 mg cholesterol, 6 g dietary fiber, 138 mg sodium

desserts

chocolate–peanut butter cheesecake

Peanut butter and chocolate have long been a winning combination, but when they're joined in a cheesecake, the result is pure bliss.

CRUST:

1½ CUPS CHOCOLATE COOKIE
CRUMBS

¼ CUP NONHYDROGENATED
MARGARINE, MELTED

FILLING:

2 PACKAGES (8 OUNCES EACH)
CREAM CHEESE OR TOFU CREAM
CHEESE, SOFTENED

¾ CUP SUGAR

½ CUP MILK OR SOY MILK, AT ROOM
TEMPERATURE

⅓ CUP CREAMY PEANUT BUTTER, AT
ROOM TEMPERATURE

½ CUP SEMISWEET CHOCOLATE
CHIPS, MELTED

FOR THE CRUST:

1. Preheat the oven to 350°F. Lightly oil an 8-inch springform pan.

2. In a bowl or food processor, combine the crumbs with the margarine and mix well. Place the crumb mixture in the bottom of the prepared pan and press it against the bottom and sides.

FOR THE FILLING:

1. In a large bowl, combine 1 package of cream cheese, $1/2$ cup of the sugar, $1/4$ cup of the milk, and the peanut butter and beat until smooth. Pour into the prepared crust and set aside.

2. In the same bowl, combine the remaining 1 package cream cheese, $1/4$ cup sugar, and $1/4$ cup milk and beat until smooth. Fold in the melted chocolate and mix until well blended.

3. Using a circular motion, pour the chocolate mixture into the peanut butter mixture. With a thin metal spatula or knife, swirl the different colored mixtures around to create a marbled pattern.

4. Bake until firm, about 45 to 50 minutes. Remove the cake from the oven and let it cool completely at room temperature. Refrigerate for several hours before serving.

SERVES 10

PER SERVING: 453 calories, 8 g protein, 38 g carbohydrates, 31 g total fat, 15 g saturated fat, 51 mg cholesterol, 2 g dietary fiber, 306 mg sodium

peach pie with peanut crumb topping

This pie is a delicious way to enjoy fresh ripe peaches. The crumb topping, made with peanut butter and rolled oats, is more healthful than using a double pie crust, so you won't feel guilty going back for seconds. If your peaches are not very sweet, you may want to add a little more sugar.

CRUST:

1 CUP ALL-PURPOSE FLOUR

1/2 TEASPOON SALT

1/3 CUP NONHYDROGENATED MARGARINE, CUT INTO SMALL PIECES

2 TABLESPOONS ICE WATER, OR MORE IF NEEDED

FILLING:

1 TABLESPOON ALL-PURPOSE FLOUR

6 FRESH RIPE PEACHES, PEELED, PITTED, AND SLICED

2 TABLESPOONS PACKED LIGHT BROWN SUGAR

1 TABLESPOON FRESH LEMON JUICE

1/4 TEASPOON GROUND CINNAMON

1/8 TEASPOON GROUND ALLSPICE

TOPPING:

1/3 CUP ALL-PURPOSE FLOUR

1/3 CUP PACKED LIGHT BROWN SUGAR

1/4 CUP OLD-FASHIONED ROLLED OATS

1/4 CUP PEANUT BUTTER

1 TABLESPOON NONHYDROGENATED MARGARINE, CUT INTO SMALL PIECES

1/4 TEASPOON GROUND CINNAMON

1/8 TEASPOON GROUND ALLSPICE

FOR THE CRUST:

1. Combine the flour and salt in a bowl. Add the margarine and use a pastry blender to mix until crumbly. Add enough ice water to form a dough, starting with 2 tablespoons and adding more if needed.

2. Roll out into a circle to fit a 9-inch pie plate. Arrange the dough in the pie plate, crimping the edges.

3. Preheat the oven to 375°F.

FOR THE FILLING:

1. In a large bowl, combine the flour, peaches, sugar, lemon juice, cinnamon, and allspice.

2. Mix gently and pour into the prepared crust. Set aside.

FOR THE TOPPING:

1. In a small bowl, combine the flour, sugar, oats, peanut butter, margarine, cinnamon, and allspice. Use a pastry blender to mix until crumbly.

2. Sprinkle the topping over the peach mixture and bake until the fruit is bubbly and the topping is browned, about 40 minutes. Serve warm or at room temperature.

SERVES 8

PER SERVING: 270 calories, 6 g protein, 31 g carbohydrates, 14 g total fat, 4 g saturated fat, 0 mg cholesterol, 3 g dietary fiber, 268 mg sodium

apple-peanut crumble

Try this homey dessert the next time you're in the mood for apple pie but want to avoid the labor of a pie crust.

3/4 CUP LIGHT BROWN SUGAR

1/2 CUP OLD-FASHIONED ROLLED OATS

1/4 CUP ALL-PURPOSE FLOUR

1/4 CUP PEANUT BUTTER

2 TABLESPOONS NONHYDROGENATED MARGARINE

1 TEASPOON CINNAMON

4 LARGE GRANNY SMITH OR OTHER COOKING APPLES

1 TABLESPOON FRESH LEMON JUICE

1/4 TEASPOON ALLSPICE

1 TABLESPOON CORNSTARCH

1. In a small bowl, combine 1/4 cup of the sugar, the oats, flour, peanut butter, margarine, and 1/2 teaspoon of the cinnamon. Use a pastry blender to mix until crumbly. Set aside.

2. Preheat the oven to 375°F. Peel, core, and thinly slice the apples and place them in a large bowl. Add the lemon juice, allspice, cornstarch, and the remaining 1/2 cup sugar and 1/2 teaspoon cinnamon. Stir to mix well, then spoon the apple mixture into a shallow baking dish or 10-inch deep-dish pie plate. Sprinkle the reserved topping evenly over the apples.

3. Bake until the apples are tender and the topping is golden brown, about 45 minutes. Serve warm or at room temperature.

SERVES 8

PER SERVING: 192 calories, 3 g protein, 29 g carbohydrates, 8 g total fat, 2 g saturated fat, 0 mg cholesterol, 6 g dietary fiber, 61 mg sodium

all things peanut butter

For more information on the beloved spread, check out the Web site

www.peanutbutterlovers.com, published by the Peanut Advisory

Board, a nonprofit association that represents many of America's

peanut farmers.

black-bottom peanut butter freezer pie (photo on page 116)

This richly decadent peanut butter pie is quick and easy to make but looks and tastes like it took all day to prepare.

CRUST:

1½ CUPS FAT-FREE CHOCOLATE COOKIE CRUMBS

¼ CUP NONHYDROGENATED MARGARINE, MELTED

FILLING:

1 QUART REGULAR OR SOY VANILLA ICE CREAM, SOFTENED

¾ CUP CREAMY PEANUT BUTTER

¼ CUP CHOPPED PEANUTS

1 CUP CHOCOLATE CURLS

FOR THE CRUST:

1. Lightly coat a 9-inch pie plate with nonstick cooking spray.

2. In a medium bowl, combine the cookie crumbs and the margarine until well blended. Transfer to the prepared pan and press the crumb mixture onto the bottom and sides. Set aside.

FOR THE FILLING:

1. In a large bowl, combine the ice cream with the peanut butter, mixing until well blended. Spoon into the prepared crust. Freeze for 4 to 6 hours or overnight.

2. When ready to serve, let the pie sit at room temperature for 5 minutes. Sprinkle the chopped peanuts in the center of the pie and the chocolate curls along the outer edge.

SERVES 8

PER SERVING: 394 calories, 10 g protein, 34 g carbohydrates, 28 g total fat, 7 g saturated fat, 2 mg cholesterol, 3 g dietary fiber, 158 mg sodium

fantasy brownies

The happy marriage of peanut butter, chocolate, and bananas produces wonderful results in these rich, moist brownies.

1 LARGE RIPE BANANA

1/3 CUP PEANUT BUTTER

1 TEASPOON VANILLA EXTRACT

4 OUNCES SEMISWEET CHOCOLATE

3/4 CUP SUGAR

1/4 CUP NONHYDROGENATED MARGARINE

1 CUP ALL-PURPOSE FLOUR

1 TEASPOON BAKING POWDER

1/2 CUP CHOPPED DRY-ROASTED PEANUTS

1. Preheat the oven to 350°F. Lightly grease the bottom only of an 8-inch square baking pan. Set aside.

2. In a blender or food processor, combine the banana, peanut butter, and vanilla and puree until smooth. Set aside.

3. Place the chocolate in a small heatproof bowl and melt over a small saucepan of simmering water, stirring occasionally, until melted. Keep warm over very low heat.

4. In a medium bowl, combine the sugar and margarine and beat until well blended. Beat in the reserved banana mixture and blend well. Add the flour and baking powder and beat until combined. Spoon the batter into the prepared pan, then swirl in the reserved chocolate and the peanuts to create a marbled effect.

5. Bake until the top springs back when touched, 25 to 30 minutes. Cool completely in the pan before cutting.

MAKES 16

PER BROWNIE: 197 calories, 4 g protein, 24 g carbohydrates, 10 g total fat, 3 g saturated fat, 0 mg cholesterol, 2 g dietary fiber, 69 mg sodium

double-dare peanut butter cake

Peanut butter lovers will appreciate the double indulgence of this peanut butter cake topped with peanut butter icing.

CAKE:

1 1/2 CUPS UNBLEACHED ALL-PURPOSE FLOUR

2 TEASPOONS BAKING POWDER

1/4 TEASPOON SALT

3/4 CUP PEANUT BUTTER

1/3 CUP NONHYDROGENATED MARGARINE, SOFTENED

1 CUP LIGHT BROWN SUGAR

2 EGGS OR BLENDED EGG SUBSTITUTE FOR 2 EGGS (SEE NOTE, PAGE 109)

1/2 CUP MILK OR SOY MILK

1 TEASPOON VANILLA EXTRACT

ICING:

1 1/2 CUPS CONFECTIONERS' SUGAR

1/2 CUP CREAMY PEANUT BUTTER

1/4 CUP MILK OR SOY MILK

3 TABLESPOONS NONHYDROGENATED MARGARINE, SOFTENED

1 TEASPOON VANILLA EXTRACT

1 CUP CHOCOLATE CURLS (OPTIONAL)

FOR THE CAKE:

1. Preheat the oven to 350°F. Lightly grease an 8-inch baking pan and set aside.

2. In a medium bowl, combine the flour, baking powder, and salt.

3. In a large bowl, using an electric mixer, cream together the peanut butter, margarine, and sugar until blended. Beat in the eggs, milk, and vanilla until blended. Add the flour mixture and mix on low speed until evenly blended.

4. Transfer the batter to the prepared pan and bake until done, about 30 minutes, or until a tester comes out clean. Let the cake cool completely before icing.

FOR THE ICING:

1. Combine the sugar, peanut butter, milk, margarine, and vanilla in a food processor and blend until smooth and creamy.

2. Refrigerate at least 1 hour before using to allow it to firm up. Then ice the cake and sprinkle the top with the chocolate curls, if using.

SERVES 10

PER SERVING: 399 calories, 9 g protein, 42 g carbohydrates, 23 g total fat, 6 g saturated fat, 44 mg cholesterol, 2 g dietary fiber, 318 mg sodium

peanut butter biscotti

These biscotti make a nice, not-too-sweet accompaniment to a cup of coffee or tea in the afternoon. For a more decadent version, glaze the tops with melted chocolate.

$2/3$ CUP SUGAR

$1/3$ CUP NONHYDROGENATED MARGARINE, SOFTENED

$1/4$ CUP CRUNCHY PEANUT BUTTER

2 EGGS OR BLENDED EGG SUBSTITUTE FOR 2 EGGS (SEE NOTE, PAGE 109)

1 TEASPOON VANILLA EXTRACT

2 CUPS ALL-PURPOSE FLOUR

$1^1/2$ TEASPOONS BAKING POWDER

$1/4$ CUP CHOPPED PEANUTS

1. Preheat the oven to 350°F. Lightly oil a baking sheet.

2. In a mixing bowl, cream the sugar into the margarine and peanut butter until well blended. Blend in the eggs and vanilla. Mix in the flour and baking powder, then stir in the chopped peanuts. Chill the dough for 10 minutes.

3. Form the dough into a slab about 1 inch high and place it on the prepared baking sheet. Flatten slightly. Bake until golden brown, 25 to 30 minutes, or until a toothpick inserted into the center comes out clean. Remove from the oven and reduce the temperature to 300°F.

4. Cool for 10 minutes, then cut into $1/2$-inch-thick slices. Place the sliced biscotti on their sides on an ungreased baking sheet and bake for 10 minutes. Cool completely before storing in an airtight container, where they will keep for up to 2 weeks.

MAKES 12

PER BISCOTTI: 219 calories, 5 g protein, 28 g carbohydrates, 10 g total fat, 3 g saturated fat, 35 mg cholesterol, 1 g dietary fiber, 125 mg sodium

working for peanuts

Most of the 16,000 peanut farms in the United States operate in nine states and grow an average of 98 acres of peanuts (per farm) each year.

coconut-peanut butter wonton cups with fresh mango

A creamy peanut filling, studded with refreshing bits of mango, is nestled in crisp wonton cups and garnished with sliced mango and mint in this dazzling and different dessert. Use very ripe, sweet mangoes for the best results.

8 WONTON WRAPPERS

PEANUT OIL OR OTHER LIGHT FLAVORLESS OIL

2 RIPE MANGOES

1 CUP UNSWEETENED COCONUT MILK

1/2 CUP SUGAR

1 1/2 TABLESPOONS CORNSTARCH DISSOLVED IN 2 TABLESPOONS WATER

1/3 CUP PEANUT BUTTER

MINT LEAVES

1. Preheat the oven to 375°F. Lightly brush the wonton wrappers on both sides with a small amount of oil. Gently press each wrapper into the cups of a muffin tin. Bake until lightly crisped, 6 to 8 minutes. Remove from the oven and set aside to cool.

2. Chop 1 mango and set aside. Cut the remaining mango into thin slices and set aside.

3. In a small saucepan, heat the coconut milk and sugar just to a boil, stirring to dissolve the sugar. Reduce the heat to low and stir in the cornstarch mixture, stirring to thicken. Add the peanut butter and blend until smooth. Transfer the mixture to a bowl and fold in the chopped mango. Refrigerate until chilled.

4. When ready to serve, spoon the chilled filling into the wonton cups and arrange on dessert plates. Garnish with the sliced mango and mint leaves.

SERVES 8

PER WONTON: 256 calories, 5 g protein, 32 g carbohydrates, 14 g total fat, 7 g saturated fat, 1 mg cholesterol, 3 g dietary fiber, 76 mg sodium

three-nut butter cookies

If you don't have chunky peanut butter, you can use creamy peanut butter and add ¼ cup chopped peanuts with the other nuts in this recipe.

2 CUPS UNBLEACHED ALL-PURPOSE FLOUR

1 TEASPOON BAKING POWDER

½ TEASPOON SALT

1 CUP CHUNKY PEANUT BUTTER

⅔ CUP LIGHT BROWN SUGAR

½ CUP NONHYDROGENATED MARGARINE, SOFTENED

1 TEASPOON VANILLA EXTRACT

⅓ CUP CHOPPED WALNUTS

⅓ CUP SLIVERED ALMONDS

1. Preheat the oven to 350°F. In a medium bowl, combine the flour, baking powder, and salt.

2. In a bowl or food processor, combine the peanut butter, sugar, margarine, and vanilla and blend until smooth. Add to the flour mixture and stir briskly until just blended. Stir in the walnuts and almonds.

3. Drop the dough by the tablespoonful onto nonstick baking sheets. With the tines of a fork, press lightly into the tops of the cookies to flatten slightly.

4. Bake until lightly browned but still slightly soft, 10 to 12 minutes. Cool completely. These can be stored in an airtight container for up to 3 days (if they last that long, they're so good).

MAKES 24

PER COOKIE: 150 calories, 4 g protein, 10 g carbohydrates, 11 g total fat, 2 g saturated fat, 0 mg cholesterol, 1 g dietary fiber, 126 mg sodium

oatmeal-peanut bars

These tasty treats are quick and easy to put together in the food processor and bake in just 20 minutes.

½ CUP NONHYDROGENATED MARGARINE

½ CUP LIGHT BROWN SUGAR

⅓ CUP PEANUT BUTTER

1 TEASPOON VANILLA EXTRACT

2 CUPS OLD-FASHIONED ROLLED OATS

¼ CUP ALL-PURPOSE FLOUR

⅓ CUP SWEETENED DRIED CRANBERRIES

¼ CUP CHOPPED UNSALTED ROASTED PEANUTS

4 OUNCES SEMISWEET CHOCOLATE CHIPS, MELTED (OPTIONAL)

1. Preheat the oven to 350°F. Lightly grease an 8-inch square baking pan.

2. In a food processor, combine the margarine, sugar, peanut butter, and vanilla until blended. Add the oats, flour, cranberries, and peanuts and pulse until well combined. Press the mixture into the bottom of the prepared pan and bake for 20 minutes.

3. Remove from the oven and drizzle with the melted chocolate, if using. Cool completely in the pan, then cut into 2¾ × 2-inch bars.

MAKES 12

PER BAR: 221 calories, 5 g protein, 19 g carbohydrates, 14 g total fat, 4 g saturated fat, 0 mg cholesterol, 3 g dietary fiber, 104 mg sodium

east coast/west coast

On the East Coast, the peanut butter of choice is creamy, while on the

West Coast, people prefer crunchy-style peanut butter.

silken peanut butter pudding

This silky smooth pudding is a delicious way to sneak heart-healthy tofu into your recipes. For an elegant presentation, serve in martini glasses garnished with chopped peanuts, chocolate curls, and a red-ripe strawberry or a few raspberries. Alternately, pour the pudding into a prepared chocolate cookie crumb crust for a decadently luscious pie.

8 OUNCES PEANUT BUTTER BAKING CHIPS

1 CUP SILKEN TOFU

½ CUP PEANUT BUTTER

2½ TABLESPOONS SUGAR

2 TABLESPOONS MILK OR SOY MILK

1 TEASPOON VANILLA EXTRACT

1. Melt the peanut butter chips over a double boiler.

2. Meanwhile, combine the tofu, peanut butter, sugar, milk, and vanilla in a blender or food processor. Add the melted chips and process until thoroughly blended.

3. Pour the mixture into 4 dessert glasses and refrigerate for at least 2 hours before serving.

SERVES 4

PER SERVING: 300 calories, 12 g protein, 18 g carbohydrates, 22 g total fat, 3 g saturated fat, 1 mg cholesterol, 3 g dietary fiber, 81 mg sodium

note: If you can't find peanut butter baking chips, you can use white baking chocolate instead, with excellent results.

grilled fruit satays with pineapple-coconut peanut sauce

Vary the fruit in this dessert according to the season and your preference—bananas, apricots, and peaches are good choices. If using bamboo skewers, be sure to soak them in water for 30 minutes to prevent burning.

SAUCE:

2 TABLESPOONS NONHYDROGENATED MARGARINE

1/2 CUP LIGHT BROWN SUGAR

1/2 CUP PEANUT BUTTER

1/2 CUP PINEAPPLE JUICE

1/2 CUP UNSWEETENED COCONUT MILK

FRUIT:

3 RIPE PLUMS, HALVED, PITTED, AND CUT INTO 1½-INCH CHUNKS

1 PINEAPPLE, PEELED, CORED, AND CUT INTO 1½-INCH CHUNKS

1 CUP HULLED STRAWBERRIES

SUGAR

FOR THE SAUCE:

1. Melt the margarine in a small saucepan over medium heat. Add the sugar and stir to dissolve. Stir in the peanut butter, then add the pineapple juice and coconut milk, stirring constantly. Reduce the heat to low and simmer for 1 minute.

2. Keep the sauce warm while you grill the fruit.

FOR THE FRUIT:

1. Thread the plums, pineapple, and strawberries onto skewers in an alternating pattern. Sprinkle with a little sugar and grill them on both sides, just until grill marks start to appear, about 5 minutes.

2. Arrange the skewered fruit on 4 plates along with small dipping bowls of the warm sauce.

SERVES 4

PER SERVING: 475 calories, 11 g protein, 42 g carbohydrates, 33 g total fat, 11 g saturated fat, 0 mg cholesterol, 7 g dietary fiber, 157 mg sodium

more sweet treats

too easy chocolate-peanut butter fudge

This fudge is "too easy" not to make on a regular basis! It firms up very quickly, so be sure to get it into the pan right away.

8 OUNCES SEMISWEET
CHOCOLATE, COARSELY CHOPPED,
OR CHOCOLATE CHIPS

1 CUP PEANUT BUTTER

1/2 CUP NONHYDROGENATED
MARGARINE

1 CUP CONFECTIONERS' SUGAR

1 TEASPOON VANILLA EXTRACT

1. Lightly grease an 8-inch square baking pan.

2. Place the chocolate, peanut butter, and margarine in a heatproof bowl and set it over a saucepan of simmering water, stirring until the chocolate melts and the mixture is smooth.

3. Turn off the heat and whisk in the sugar and vanilla until smooth and well blended.

4. Scrape the mixture into the prepared pan and cool until firm. Cut into squares. Keep refrigerated.

MAKES 36

PER PIECE: 120 calories, 2 g protein, 9 g carbohydrates, 9 g total fat, 3 g saturated fat, 0 mg cholesterol, 1 g dietary fiber, 44 mg sodium

runner peanuts

Of the four types of peanuts grown in the United States (Runner, Spanish, Valencia, and Virginia), Runners are preferred for peanut butter. Grown mostly in Alabama, Florida, and Georgia, Runners roast evenly because they are uniform in size.

peanut butter cups—my way

For bite-size versions of this delicious treat, use small paper candy cups instead of the cupcake liners.

½ CUP NONHYDROGENATED MARGARINE

1 CUP CREAMY PEANUT BUTTER

½ TEASPOON VANILLA EXTRACT

¾ CUP CONFECTIONERS' SUGAR

1 PACKAGE (12 OUNCES) SEMISWEET CHOCOLATE CHIPS

1. Melt the margarine in a medium saucepan over low heat. Stir in the peanut butter and vanilla until well blended. Remove from the heat and stir in the sugar. Mix well until thoroughly combined, then refrigerate.

2. Place the chocolate chips in a heatproof bowl and set it over a saucepan of simmering water until the chocolate is melted.

3. Use a small brush to coat the chocolate over the bottom and about ½ inch up the sides of 12 paper cupcake liners. Reserve the remaining chocolate. Refrigerate the cups until firm, about 10 minutes.

4. Scoop out about 2 tablespoons of the peanut butter mixture and shape into a ball. Flatten the ball into a disk and place inside one of the chilled chocolate-lined cups. Repeat until all the cups are filled. Spoon 2 teaspoons of the remaining melted chocolate over the top of each cup. Refrigerate until firm.

MAKES 12

PER CANDY: 394 calories, 8 g protein, 33 g carbohydrates, 29 g total fat, 10 g saturated fat, 0 mg cholesterol, 3 g dietary fiber, 132 mg sodium

christina's coconut chocolate peanut butter truffles (photo on page 136, pictured with Orange Decadence Truffles)

When you love chocolate, peanut butter, and coconut, there's only one thing to do—make these lovely and decadent truffles, created by one of my recipe testers, Christina O'Brien.

⅓ CUP SEMISWEET CHOCOLATE CHIPS

⅓ CUP CREAMY PEANUT BUTTER

3 TABLESPOONS COCONUT MILK

⅔ CUP CONFECTIONERS' SUGAR

⅓ CUP PLUS 1 CUP FINELY SHREDDED UNSWEETENED COCONUT

1. Place the chocolate in a heatproof bowl and set it over a small saucepan of simmering water until the chocolate melts. (Or melt the chocolate chips by placing them in a small microwaveable bowl and microwave on high for about 1½ minutes, or just until the chocolate is completely melted.) Add the peanut butter and coconut milk and blend until smooth and creamy.

2. Place the chocolate mixture, sugar, and ⅓ cup shredded coconut into a food processor and process until well combined.

3. Shape the mixture into 1-inch balls and roll them in the 1 cup coconut. Place them on a platter or a baking sheet. Cover and refrigerate until ready to use.

MAKES 12

PER TRUFFLE: 179 calories, 3 g protein, 16 g carbohydrates, 13 g total fat, 8 g saturated fat, 0 mg cholesterol, 3 g dietary fiber, 20 mg sodium

orange decadence truffles

(photo on page 136, pictured with Christina's Coconut Chocolate Peanut Butter Truffles)

When you combine orange liqueur with chocolate and peanut butter, the result is pure decadence. These luscious morsels are easy to make and sublimely delicious. Serve the truffles in gold foil paper candy cups for an elegant presentation.

½ CUP CREAMY PEANUT BUTTER

¼ CUP NONHYDROGENATED MARGARINE

2 CUPS CONFECTIONERS' SUGAR

½ CUP UNSWEETENED COCOA

1½ TABLESPOONS GRAND MARNIER OR OTHER ORANGE LIQUEUR

1 TABLESPOON FAT-FREE HALF-AND-HALF OR SOY MILK

1 TEASPOON FINELY GRATED ORANGE ZEST

3 TABLESPOONS COCOA (OPTIONAL)

1. In a food processor, combine the peanut butter, margarine, sugar, cocoa, orange liqueur, half-and-half, and orange zest. Process until well blended.

2. Shape the mixture into 1-inch balls and place them on a platter or a baking sheet. Roll in cocoa, if using. Cover and refrigerate to firm up. Keep refrigerated until ready to use.

MAKES 24

PER TRUFFLE: 109 calories, 2 g protein, 15 g carbohydrates, 5 g total fat, 1 g saturated fat, 0 mg cholesterol, 1 g dietary fiber, 33 mg sodium

peanut butter pinwheels

This old-fashioned candy, sometimes called flitch, was a favorite in the coal region of northeastern Pennsylvania where I grew up. You can cook the potato either in the microwave or the oven. (Boiling will make it too watery.) You will need about ½ cup of mashed potato. The amount of confectioners' sugar needed will depend on the amount of moisture in the potato. The drier the potato, the less sugar you will need to form the dough. To be safe, I usually keep a backup box of sugar in the pantry.

1 SMALL POTATO, COOKED, PEELED, AND MASHED TO EQUAL ½ CUP

1 BOX (16 OUNCES) CONFECTIONERS' SUGAR, OR MORE

1 CUP CREAMY PEANUT BUTTER, AT ROOM TEMPERATURE

1. Place the mashed potato in a bowl. Mix in the sugar a little at a time, until the mixture reaches a doughlike consistency.

2. Arrange a piece of plastic wrap on a flat work surface and sprinkle a small amount of confectioners' sugar on it. Place the dough on the sugar and top with a little more sugar and another piece of plastic wrap. Roll the mixture out to ¼-inch thickness. Remove the top layer of plastic and discard.

3. Spread the peanut butter on top of the dough, then roll up (using the plastic wrap as a guide) into a round cylinder. Cover and refrigerate until chilled, about 30 minutes. (The cylinder may flatten out a bit while it cools, so you may need to reshape it slightly about halfway through the chilling process.) Cut the roll crosswise into ¼-inch-thick slices.

MAKES 30

PER PIECE: 122 calories, 2 g protein, 18 g carbohydrates, 5 g total fat, 1 g saturated fat, 0 mg cholesterol, 1 g dietary fiber, 20 mg sodium

dogs love peanut butter, too!

If you want to make something special for your best friend, try this yummy doggie treat recipe from Kelli Polsinelli of Dogs Own Pantry, an online gourmet dog treat company at www.dogsownpantry.ca. They're made with such delicious, wholesome ingredients that your four-legger may not be the only one begging for these treats—Kelli says her daughter loves them too.

peanut butter doggie treats

2 CUPS WHOLE WHEAT FLOUR

$^3/_4$ CUP PEANUT BUTTER

1 BANANA, MASHED

$^1/_4$ CUP WHEAT GERM

$^1/_2$ CUP SOY MILK

$^1/_4$ CUP CANOLA OIL

1. Preheat the oven to 350°F. Lightly grease a baking sheet.

2. Mix together the flour, peanut butter, banana, wheat germ, soy milk, and oil until evenly moist but not sticky. Knead until smooth.

3. Roll out the dough and cut into shapes with your favorite cutters and arrange on the prepared baking sheet. Bake until lightly browned, 12 to 15 minutes, or a little longer if your pup prefers a crunchy cookie. Cool completely.

MAKES ABOUT 12

Index

Note: **Boldfaced** page references indicate photographs.

Conversion Chart

These equivalents have been slightly rounded to make measuring easier.

VOLUME MEASUREMENTS

US	Imperial	Metric
1/4 tsp	–	1 ml
1/2 tsp	–	2 ml
1 tsp	–	5 ml
1 Tbsp	–	15 ml
2 Tbsp (1 oz)	1 fl oz	30 ml
1/4 cup (2 oz)	2 fl oz	60 ml
1/3 cup (3 oz)	3 fl oz	80 ml
1/2 cup (4 oz)	4 fl oz	120 ml
2/3 cup (5 oz)	5 fl oz	160 ml
3/4 cup (6 oz)	6 fl oz	180 ml
1 cup (8 oz)	8 fl oz	240 ml

WEIGHT MEASUREMENTS

US	Metric
1 oz	30 g
2 oz	60 g
4 oz (1/4 lb)	115 g
5 oz (1/3 lb)	145 g
6 oz	170 g
7 oz	200 g
8 oz (1/2 lb)	230 g
10 oz	285 g
12 oz (3/4 lb)	340 g
14 oz	400 g
16 oz (1 lb)	455 g
2.2 lb	1 kg

LENGTH MEASUREMENTS

US	Metric
1/4"	0.6 cm
1/2"	1.25 cm
1"	2.5 cm
2"	5 cm
4"	11 cm
6"	15 cm
8"	20 cm
10"	25 cm
12" (1')	30 cm

PAN SIZES

US	Metric
8" cake pan	20 × 4 cm sandwich or cake tin
9" cake pan	23 × 3.5 cm sandwich or cake tin
11" × 7" baking pan	28 × 18 cm baking tin
13" × 9" baking pan	32.5 × 23 cm baking tin
15" × 10" baking pan	38 × 25.5 cm baking tin (Swiss roll tin)
1 1/2 qt baking dish	1.5 liter baking dish
2 qt baking dish	2 liter baking dish
2 qt rectangular baking dish	30 × 19 cm baking dish
9" pie plate	22 × 4 or 23 × 4 cm pie plate
7" or 8" springform pan	18 or 20 cm springform or loose-bottom cake tin
9" × 5" loaf pan	23 × 13 cm or 2 lb narrow loaf tin or pâté tin

TEMPERATURES

Fahrenheit	Centigrade	Gas
140°	60°	–
160°	70°	–
180°	80°	–
225°	105°	1/4
250°	120°	1/2
275°	135°	1
300°	150°	2
325°	160°	3
350°	180°	4
375°	190°	5
400°	200°	6
425°	220°	7
450°	230°	8
475°	245°	9
500°	260°	–